"I have known the Schoenhoffs for four decades. Heinz and Elsie were pastoring in Canada, were missionaries in YWAM for many years and are now teaching at a university in Korea. They are not only a man and woman of God, but they have raised their own children to love God. They have lived out their message and their marriage based on Christian Biblical principles. Their rich lives and relationships will enrich your life as you read and learn from them."

Dr. Loren Cunningham,
Founder of Youth With A Mission (YWAM)

"I had the privilege of being Heinz' pastor early in my ministry. I was impressed then with his wisdom, humility, gentle spirit, and firm convictions. You will hear all these qualities come through as you read this book. This book is unique, in that it presents biblical truth about marriage that is also documented with research and illustrated through years of wise counseling. One of my core convictions is that *nothing changes anyone but the word of God applied by the Spirit of God.*

This book has the potential of changing your life."

Dr. Ken Hemphill.
*Former President of Southwestern Seminary
and current Director of the Center for Church Planting and
Revitalization, North Greenville University*

"Since I have known Heinz and Elsie for many years, I was excited when asked to write an endorsement for this book. I have seen their ministry in families' lives here in Hawaii and have heard of its effectiveness in other countries. I have recommended people to them for counseling without reservations. I knew they would give solid counseling based upon scriptural principles. Most of all, I knew Heinz would demonstrate a caring and loving attitude as hurting couples would work through their family problems.

I encourage any couple preparing for marriage to read through the book and discuss it together. Newlyweds would also gain helpful insights to guide their marriage and family. I know that people who have been married for many years would find their relationships strengthened as well. Thank you, Heinz, for putting some of your teachings into a written form."

Dr. Bob Duffer,
Pastor and former Director of Missions for the Neighbor Islands Baptist Associations of Hawaii, Southern Baptist Convention, USA

"At the beginning of creation, God *made them male and female. For this reason a man will leave his father and mother and be united to his wife, and the two will become one flesh.* So they are no longer two, but one flesh. Therefore what God has joined together, let no one separate." (Mark 10:6-9)

Marriage is the living gospel that God has given to us. Yet, there are many Christians today that struggle due to the essence of the gospel being watered-down by worldly values. In this book, written by Professor Heinz Schoenhoff, you will encounter a husband and wife perfectly one in Christ, and the Kingdom of God and family that they create. As the salt is a mere three percent of the ocean yet brings life into the vast body of water, may all who read this book grow Godly families and become the salt in these times in need of much hope."

Dr. Young-Gil Kim
President of Handong Global University, Retired
Pohang, South Korea

MARRIAGE CLASS

Learning God's Dynamic Design for Family

To Daniel,
Your future is secure
in God's hands
Jer. 29:11

HEINZ W. SCHOENHOFF

DEDICATION

I dedicate this book to Bob Slosser
who first encouraged me to write.

ACKNOWLEDGEMENTS

Warm thanks to Tim and Yukie Ohashi,
who made space available for me to write
at Volcano on the Big Island of Hawaii.

Special thanks to Stephen and Derek, my sons,
for their consistent, extremely valuable input
and encouragement.

Most of all I thank my precious wife
for the hundreds of things she did
to make this book come about.

CONTENTS

CONTENTS 11
PREFACE 13
FORWARD 16
1. In the Beginning 21
2. The Enemy of the Family 27
3. Assessing the Damage 37
4. Cleaving or Leaving 43
5. Strongholds to Demolish 51
6. The Weapons of Our Warfare 59
7. Becoming One 65
8. Train Up Your Child...71
9. Positions in the Family 83
10. God's Social Microcosm 91
11. Hope for Families in Disarray 99
12. The Heart of the Family..107
13. Communication 111
14. The Compatibility Factor..117
15. The Function of Beams..121
16. Dealing with Adversity 127
17. Domestic Violence...139
18. The Family and Work...147
19. Streets Paved with Gold..153
20. Sex and Marriage 161
21. Love Never Fails 167

PREFACE

In these opening decades of the 21st century, terrible forces are at work around the world, presenting unprecedented challenges for followers of Jesus Christ. Social and economic unrest roil the globe, spawning political and military conflict within and between nations on every continent. No part of humanity has been spared the turmoil as news and information can now circumnavigate the planet with the speed of light and the click of a button. Truly this is a time of *wars and rumors of wars*. Traditional Judeo-Christian societies in the West have grown increasingly secularized and *multi-culturalized*. The faith of many has grown cold. Animosity from neo-pagan, scientific materialist and other anti-Christian forces has increased steadily since Nietzsche's mistaken and pre-mature declaration (ironic in hindsight) that God had died. But though God has not died, Nietzsche represented a great turning away from him in the West and the world. Now, after the rise and fall of great non-Christian ideologies in the 20th century, new battle lines have been drawn and great shifts of political power and ideological influence are again underway.

In Europe and the former Soviet Union, Islam, nationalism, and environmentalism compete to fill the void left by the collapse of communism. In America, with the gradual disintegration of the Judeo-Christian consensus on which it was founded, resurgent new forms of socialism,

13

feminism, and sexual deviancy are being coercively *"normalized"* by activist minorities with aggressive social engineering agendas, infiltrating centers of power and influence and co-opting institutions of government and education. Others in America and elsewhere have noted these trends. American political scientist Dr. Stephen Baskerville has written that in the context of all these movements and forces so hostile to Christianity, the greatest danger now is to the family, and of all the threats it faces, the most dire is sexual radicalism. Since the 1960s, the agenda of sexual radicalism has come to exercise not just great influence but increasingly coercive control over public life in the Western world, giving rise to what some have called *sexual totalitarianism.* This bodes ill for American society, particularly children and families. It also bodes ill for the rest of the world, for whom America has been a refuge from oppressive and tyrannical governing systems.

My father was born into post-WWII Germany at a time also marked by turmoil and social chaos. The youngest son of a Christian family of five children, his personal heritage included early awareness of both the blessings of a solid family and the stresses and dangers to Christian families in today's world. Since then, he has dedicated his life to understanding human relationships and to working to help restore damaged lives, marriages and families, including his own. He has done so professionally through the judicial and social services institutions of the government, through pastoral Christian ministry and missionary service, as well as through private counseling practice and university level teaching and administration. With my firsthand experience of the lessons he's learned and taught others over the years, I can earnestly vouch for his sincerity and whole-hearted devotion to promoting God's design and vision for family.

This book represents a life of learning, doing and teaching. It is a vital restatement for this time of the age-old truths about what family was created to be and can be today. It should serve as a source of learning and inspiration and encouragement to us all.

Stephen A. Schoenhoff, Esq

FORWARD

In the late 1950's a determined young girl courageously escaped from East Germany to the free country of West Germany. She had disappeared from a professional international convention, crossed the border by night, risking her life in the process, and made her way to Wolfsburg, a town only six miles from the East German border. Not knowing anybody, Natasha asked for directions to a leader of a Baptist Church and that's how the girl came to stay at our place. My father was the founder and elder of the Baptist church, so, along with a number of other devastated refugees during those difficult decades after WWII, Natasha spent the first few months living with us. Eventually, she got a job in her profession and found her own accommodations. But during the time she had lived with us, she had become a close friend of my younger sister.

One of my dreams in my growing up years was to immigrate to Canada, *'the land of unlimited opportunities'*, as it was known in Germany. I had spent many hours dreaming of the wide-open prairies, the vast tundra of the North West Territories, and the rugged mountains of British Columbia. Many of my school writing assignments had had themes of the early Canadian West. I determined to make my dream come true at the first opportunity.

So it was in 1963, that my younger sister and I left Germany to follow our dreams, trailing other siblings who had already moved to Canada. We arrived in Toronto, where

I had to quickly adjust my teenage dreams to the reality of a buzzing cosmopolitan city.

Now here is the story I want to tell: My sister wrote glowing reports of her new life in this incredible country to her friend in Germany, arousing her curiosity. Soon, her girlfriend arrived in Toronto as well. She contacted some distant relatives in Alberta, over 2000 miles to the west. When the relatives heard that Natasha was in Canada, they sent their daughter, Elsie, to fetch their East German relative to the West so they could help her. However, by the time Elsie arrived in Toronto, Natasha had already changed her mind. By then she was enjoying Toronto, a new job and new friends. This was a bit of a disappointment for the families in the West, who had been eager to meet their newly discovered relative. God had had other plans.

I was introduced to Elsie during her short visit at Christmas time and was surprised to hear of her return to Toronto later in the summer. Natasha had begged her to come help prepare her wedding, having become engaged in the meantime. It turned out that Elsie and a girlfriend from the West, decided to drive across the country in a 1958 Studebaker to find summer jobs in Toronto while helping with the wedding. And so it was that during those weeks I had the opportunity to get to know Elsie. The weeks flew by way too fast.

＊＊＊＊

Days before Elsie and her friend were to drive back to Calgary, I hit on the *spontaneous* idea of asking Elsie for a date to a live play at the prestigious Royal Alexandria Theater. Although it was at the last-minute, she happily accepted. The play was a Shakespearean comedy and must have been good, judging from the enthusiastic response of the audience. My English was totally inadequate for understanding what was going on, so I dozed through most of it. But after the performance, I suggested a late night dinner at a restaurant close by. We talked and talked well past midnight. The spark that had sprung up between us that summer now burst into flame. We knew something miraculous was in the air. As we walked to the car, I stopped, turned to Elsie and looking deeply into her beautiful brown eyes, whispered the question uppermost in my mind, "Will you marry me?"

She totally amazed me with a *'Yes'!* Two days later, I left for Queen's University in Kingston, Ontario, and Elsie left for her senior year at the University of Calgary. The ensuing months grew into an intense, daily exchange of letters.

At Christmas time, I flew to Calgary to meet Elsie's family and ask her father for her hand in marriage. They gave their assent and her aunt and uncle held an official engagement party for us. Six months later, in a beautiful summer wedding, we said our *I do's* in front of two officiating pastors and a large number of guests. The honeymoon that followed was just unbelievably fun.

****

It fascinates me to hear stories of how couples meet: their first encounter, the first look, the point at which a decision strong enough to last a lifetime is made. Of all the innumerable choices, why pick this particular girl - or this particular guy? I recently talked with a young couple, who had come for some premarital counseling sessions. Repeatedly, they said in the first ten minutes, "The way we met and started our relationship was so awesome, it could only have been God." They hit the nail right on the head. Yes, GOD is *the* Matchmaker. From the very beginning of his creation, God has been in the business of finding the right life-partners - of matchmaking.

It is simply amazing how God can move a young woman from a distant location to meet a strange, young immigrant from Germany. No expense is too great for God. After marriage, we even discovered that our parents had common acquaintances! As both of us had pursued different agendas, attraction ignited. We became forever changed when we joined our lives in matrimony. An unusual story? Not at all! It still happens in surprising ways all over the world.

Heinz W Schoenhoff

Professor of Psychology and Counseling
Handong Global University, Retired

Chapter One | In the Beginning

"So God created mankind in his own image, in the image of God he created them; male and female he created them." Genesis 1:27

The first revelation we have of God, in the Bible, is that he is the Creator. God created Adam with a physical body of bones, flesh and blood. He used dirt, as his material and shaped it with his own hands. He then breathed his own life-giving Spirit, into the nostrils of this lifeless, inanimate creature and it immediately became a living soul. It became a person, with the ability to think, express emotions, make independent choices and have self-awareness. Personhood was now introduced to the planet. We know from the Bible that God is Spirit in nature. He is Spirit and communicates with our spirit (Romans 8:16; John 4:24). Although Adam had a spirit in him, his outer shell, as a human being, was made of flesh and blood. He was the first and only human being.

It is interesting to note that in order to be a creator, you must like work. No creation would ever have been accomplished without work. So, since God created man in his likeness, He also created man with the appreciation for work. Quite naturally, therefore, the first thing Adam did was work.

God had planted a beautiful garden in Eden and the new man was to take care of the rest of Creation (Genesis 2:8, 15). God also gave Adam instructions on what to eat and what not to eat and said, "You are free to eat from any tree in the Garden; but you must not eat from the tree of the knowledge of good and evil, for when you eat of it you will surely die." (Genesis 2:16, 17)

As the Creator of this first man, one can assume that God knew what would keep Adam satisfied.

God knew from the beginning, that it was not good for the man to be alone. One essential element of being created in the image of God is the fact that man was created for companionship. After all, when God set out to create man, He said, '*Let US create man in OUR image*,' which shows the plurality of the Father, God the Son and God the Holy Spirit. In Genesis 1:2 we see that already before God spoke things into existence, "the Spirit of God was hovering over the waters." And in Colossians 1:16 and 17 we read: "For by [Christ] all things were created: things in heaven and on earth, visible and invisible, whether thrones or powers or rulers or authorities: all things were created by him and for him. He is before all things, and in him all things hold together."

****

The unity between the Father, the Son and the Holy Spirit is that remarkable quality that God wanted to transmit into the crown of His creation: mankind. It is so free of dissention and pursuit of self-will, that in it lies the secret of power and authority. Each of them is '*God*'; therefore each reflects the other without distortion. For example, Jesus said to Philip: "He who sees me, sees the Father"(John 14:9). Peter said to Ananias: "You have lied to the Holy Spirit". In the next sentence, Peter said: "You have lied to God" (Acts 5:1-4). Therefore, he who lies to God, the Father, is also lying to the Holy Spirit and to Jesus Christ. Jesus said of the Holy Spirit: "[The Holy Spirit] will not speak on his own, he will speak only what he hears."(John 16:13) We remember Jesus' prayer, "Father, if you are willing, take this cup from me; yet not my will, but yours be done." (Luke 22:42) What a picture of total submission and surrender to the will of the Father! The unity within the Godhead (known as the *Trinity*) is perfect. They are three distinct Persons, yet they are one God.

Therefore, when God spoke regarding humanity, "It is not good for man to be alone, I'll make a helper just right for him," (Genesis 2:18) it appears that it was his intention to create the same outstanding harmony between these two (and all couples), as is in the Godhead. This was God's model for marriage.

In creating the helper for Adam, God chose not to duplicate his creative process. Eve was not made from dirt, but from a portion of Adam. This time, God chose divine anesthesia as his creative method. He put Adam to sleep and surgically removed one of his ribs from his ribcage, then he shaped that rib into a person similar in appearance to Adam. When Adam awoke, God presented the new person to Adam, who immediately recognized her as someone like himself and claimed her as his own, saying, "This is now bone of my bones and flesh of my flesh; she shall be called woman, for she was taken out of man." (Genesis 2:18-23) Later, Adam gave her a personal name, Eve, because she was also the *mother of all the living*. (Genesis 3:20)

I've often wondered why God chose to do things in this way. What could have been his purpose? As I've reflected on these verses in the Bible, I've pondered on what else Adam excitedly said when God first brought Eve to him. He recognized that she was the one he had unknowingly longed for. None of the other creatures he had spent his days with had given him the needed fellowship or intimacy. By comparison, the relationship we can have with plants, animals, or trees is vastly different, shallow and impersonal. Only a human being has the ability to express the personal character of God, through compassion, generosity, mercy, creativity, thinking, responsibility, unconditional love, choices, forgiveness, kindness and self-sacrifice.

Eve was taken from the specific place in Adam's body that would make him vulnerable to life-threatening injuries. The ribcage was clearly designed to protect his heart and lungs. The lungs, the breathing apparatus, are essential for survival. They supply the body with oxygen needed for metabolism and they exhale carbon dioxide after the oxygen has done its job. The heart, that moves the blood through the whole body to assure life in every cell, would need special protection.

The rib that became Eve, was God's chosen being to enable Adam to accomplish what he could not have accomplished by himself. In Genesis 1:27, we read: "male and female he created them". Right after that, it says in verse 28: "God blessed them and said to them, 'Be fruitful and increase in number; fill the earth and subdue it. Rule over the fish of the sea and the birds of the air and over every living creature that moves on the ground.'" What an awesome assignment for this first couple! As a rib, she was to protect life; as a woman she was to give life. As a rib, she was to cover the heart; as a heart she was to be the *feeling center* or nucleus of the family.

Have you ever wondered what God could possibly have said when he blessed this first couple? It doesn't say that he blessed them in any one particular area. It seems he blessed their whole life, from the beginning to the end. All of his intentions for them were imparted into their union. By blessing Adam and Eve, God first revealed his heart for the human race. His original plan was for Man to live a full happy and purposeful life. In speaking to Adam and Eve, and future generations he might have said: "Adam and Eve, you have everything you'll need, all you could ever want. It's yours to use. Now just go and enjoy it. I have created it all for you; make the best of it."

So, God gave man his blessing to explore, research, discover, enjoy, build, multiply, cultivate, foster, nurture and develop. All of the future disciplines: sciences, discoveries, professions, business, commerce, education, occupations, communication, and many more, had their beginnings here. The stage was set for families to form, civilizations to emerge and nations to cover the earth. God spoke another word - a prophetic word - that was to affect all future generations, right through to our times, "For this reason a man will leave father and mother and be united to his wife and the two will become one flesh." (Genesis 2:24)

What did he mean when he said, *for this reason*? Without a doubt, God was referring to the transition from groom to husband in future marriages. Whenever a man would step into the position of *husband*, the one thing he would have to do was to leave his father and mother, establish his own household, and fulfill his own responsibilities. By the time a young man would take this step, he was to learn from his own father what would be involved in being a husband. And one of the main things he would have needed to learn would be to trust God the Father, to know how to hear his voice and how to obey him. Because this point is such a foundational matter for family life, we'll come back to this verse repeatedly in future chapters.

We can see why there is no question that it was God, who initiated, ordained, and blessed marriage. He set the stage for communicating his nature and ways from one generation to the next and his plan for his creation and individual lives are interwoven with the dynamic union between husband and wife.

SUMMARY

We were created by a personal, loving God in a very unique way that enables us to be a reflection of our Creator. We can think and feel and understand. We can receive love and express love. We are created with the same strong desire for relationship as is reflected in the Godhead.

Chapter Two | The Enemy of the Family

"Your enemy the devil prowls around like a roaring lion looking for someone to devour." 1 Peter 5:8

The Creator created many things not visible to us. We are limited to three dimensions. What if God, in his infinite ability, created things in multiple dimensions? In our finiteness, we are not able to think in five, ten or thirty dimensional terms. We simply can't break out of the three-dimensional space concept. It's next to impossible, for example, to think or see *spirit* unless God materializes a spirit. How significant that the Son of God, Jesus, took on human form and became the Son of Man, but then became Spirit again afterwards. Now when we think of *spirit*, we have a visual image in our mind, something we have seen before, that we can touch, define or describe.

Angels are beings created sometime before our physical universe. The Bible teaches us that among them was the most beautiful one, called "morning star, son of the dawn". The most frequently used name, though, is "Satan" which means *adversary* or *accuser*. Satan had adopted some ambitious ideas and wanted to become like God by setting his throne above

God's. In Ezekiel 28:12-19 and Isaiah 14:12-17, we are told that he didn't succeed. Jesus tells us that he was present when Satan was cast out of heaven to the earth because of his rebellion (Luke 10:18). Along with him, all the angels that had sided with him were dispelled. These fallen angels have become known to us as demons or devils. Whether or not new demons were added to the original number of fallen angels is a matter of speculation.[1]

The question many people ask is, "How did Satan succeed in infiltrating God's creation in order to begin its downfall? What strategy did he use to damage God's masterpiece, the family?" To begin with, we need to remember that God created man in his own likeness, which means that man has the ability to think for himself and make his own choices. In other words, he has a free will (within the context of creation). This is one of the truly ingenious aspects of God's work. He took the risk of having another being (like Lucifer) who would choose to stand against God, or the *opposite* – a being who would cooperate *with* God and express reciprocal love *for* God. In order to see which way man would turn, God put him to the test by allowing Satan, disguised as a serpent, to enter God's Garden of Eden.

With the scene set, Satan came in and decided to approach Eve (Adam's helper). His game plan was to see whether she knew what God had told Adam, and if so, whether she would stand firm on what she had learned. The devil spotted her fascination with the tree of the Knowledge

---

[1] While the Scriptures give no definite figures, we are told that the number of angels is very great (Daniel 7:10) Matthew 26:53; Hebrews 12:22). It appears that all angels were created at one time. No new angels are being added to the number. Angels are not subject to death or any form of extinction; therefore they do not decrease in number. Dr. Paul Eymann. http://christiananswers.net/q-acb/acb-t005.html#3

of Good and Evil. He snuck up on her and posed an innocent-sounding question: "Did God really say, 'You must not eat from any tree in the garden?'" Not suspecting that it was God's enemy who was speaking to her, she responded to the snake's pleasant voice, "We may eat fruit from the trees in the garden, but God did say, 'You must not eat fruit from the tree that is in the middle of the garden, and you must not touch it, or you will die.'" (Genesis 3:1-5) This answer told Satan that Eve had only casual knowledge of what God had originally stated. Eve had added, "You must not touch it." Therefore, Satan knew she would be a good target for deception. He moved quickly to confuse Eve and pull her to his side. Faking a superior authority, the *I know better* role, he said, "You will not surely die." This was not only distorting, but contradicting what God had said, "For God knows that when you eat of it your eyes will be opened, and you will be like God, knowing good and evil." Satan spoke with such *know-it-all* flare, that it was easy to convince Eve that God seemed to be withholding something important from her. Her initial curiosity about the tree could have been so beneficial, had she discussed it with God and her husband. But as her heart turned away from God towards Satan, she suddenly saw the tree with different eyes. Disobedience to God (beginning in the heart) seemed attractive and enticing to her: the forbidden fruit "looked good for food and pleasing to the eye, and also desirable for gaining wisdom." She took some of it and ate it, contrary to what God had told them. She also gave some to her husband, "who was with her and he ate." (Genesis 3:6)

What can we learn from this story, so far, that might help us recognize the enemy of the family, Satan, and identify his strategies? First of all, it is clear that insufficient or partial knowledge of the word of God can lead to doubt and deceitful ideas. Secondly, not verifying these ideas through the Word of God can allow information presented to us by ungodly teachers, through relatives, friends, books, movies, internet, etc., to lead us to wrong conclusions. As a result, our own abilities in the world around us, the scope of our *free* will and our moral autonomy may become exaggerated in our minds. Thirdly, in hindsight, it is obvious that for Adam not to stand between Satan and his wife was to neglect one of his primary responsibilities of protecting his wife.

A fourth point we can observe from the creation account is that Satan aroused human pride, his primary weapon, by suggesting they could be like God. Simplistic? Absurd? Yes, of course! An isolated incidence? Absolutely not! The lie has mushroomed in man's religions, ideologies, and among certain sciences. This one false notion started man's incessant restlessness, his continuous search for significance, his drive to gratify the resulting thirst for power, and a dark propensity for control. How tragic! The search for new discoveries was part of God's command to subdue the earth, and dominate it (Genesis 1:28). What had changed through this Genesis event was that man's natural curiosity and investigation turned to self-gratification. Covetousness entered God's creation and became the mainstream lifestyle. Instead of enjoying God's presence and learning from him, man became jealous of God and mainly self-absorbed with disastrous results.

After Adam and Eve had eaten of the forbidden fruit, they noticed their nakedness and felt ashamed. Until that time, the Bible said, that they "were naked, but were not ashamed" (Genesis 2:25). Having never had that feeling of shame, they related it to their nakedness. The fact is, shame is the result of an inner awareness of having a broken relationship with God through disobedience. Adam and Eve's attempt to cover their nakedness with fig leaves is a picture of how people try to cover their sins before God and one another today. We try to patch up the outward appearance of the sin, to give a good impression, when in fact God looks at the heart. In our independence from him, we hear the voice of the Holy Spirit through the sensation called *conviction,* which is registered as guilt in our conscience (John 16:8 NKJV). Man is incapable of keeping sins hidden from God or even from man. God alone can remedy the tangled web man weaves for himself.

However, God did not throw up his hands and leave. He went looking for Adam. "Where are you?" he called. Adam and Eve tried to avoid God, (a favorite human reaction to guilt). "I heard you in the garden, and I was afraid because I was naked; so I hid." (Genesis 3:10). We hide behind excuses, too. We close our eyes to the real reason for our fear or misery (sometimes for many, many years), and we rationalize like crazy, often until we even believe our own lies. How hard it is to admit our own responsibility for our actions!

"Who told you that you were naked?" God asked, "Have you eaten from the tree that I commanded you not to eat from?" (v.11) Most of the time the Lord makes it easy for us to clear our conscience. He convicts us by putting his finger on the right problem: disobedience. And what do we do? Listen to Adam's answer: "The woman you put here with me - she gave me some fruit from the tree and I ate it" (v12). Blaming, blaming! First of all, Adam's blame is put on the person closest to Adam. Secondly, he even blames God! Does that sound familiar?

During my graduate studies, I worked at an alcoholic rehabilitation center. It was my assignment to sit in on Alcoholics Anonymous counseling groups to observe and analyze the reasoning of the participants. Even to the casual on-looker, it was obvious that most of the men were having struggles accepting responsibility for their actions. One man, for example, stood up, introduced himself in AA fashion, "My name is … I'm an alcoholic…" He then proceeded to tell the group how he had had a very bad weekend. His wife had reminded him of constantly squandering the family's money. Finally, he couldn't help but go down to the bar and get drunk. You should have heard the group get on his case. They were remembering an important AA rule not to blame others. They showed no mercy. The poor guy got the message: *If you're under pressure, don't resort to old drinking habits to resolve the tension. Besides, you never blame someone else for your own actions!*

It was Adam who started the pattern. Eve heard her husband trying to wiggle his way out of his guilt. When God turned to her with *What is this you have done?*, she continued the example Adam had set. She tried to spin the facts to her advantage. "The serpent deceived me, and I ate."(v.13). There was, of course, no need for God to ask these probing questions. He knew before he had come to walk and talk with them what had happened. It was out of his love for them, that he involved them in identifying their sin, which had now been introduced into God's home for humanity, the planet Earth, through Adam and Eve's acts of disobedience. Their sin included: covetousness, disobedience, self-protection, shame, avoiding God, lying, blaming, rejection, deception, enmity with each other, not accepting responsibility for their disobedience, cover-up and fear.

The grief that God must have felt could only be understood, in a small measure, by the profound pain of loving parents who see their precious child wander off into extremely dangerous, potentially deadly, paths. In the next verses (Genesis 3:14-19), God describes the consequences of rejecting his moral order. He called them *curses* (harmful events), as opposed to *blessings* (benefits). The curses would never erase the promises God spoke out when he blessed Adam and Eve, but they set huge barriers between the couple and his blessings.

Amazingly and wonderfully, it is at this very point that God's plan of restoration begins! When God cursed the serpent (Genesis 3:15), he pronounced enmity between the serpent (Satan) and the promise-bearing nation of Israel (the woman whose off-spring would be Jesus). Jesus would crush Satan's head, but the serpent would only be able to bruise Christ's heel. We read, "And I will put enmity between you and the woman, and between your offspring and hers; he will crush your head, and you will strike his heel." (Genesis 3:15)

This is the earliest pronouncement of God's plan for reconciling human beings to Himself. What was the fallout of *the Fall,* as this first great watershed moment in human history has come to be known? Eve, the woman, the wife and the future mother, suffered considerable damage. Now motherhood became a love-hate proposition. On the one hand, motherhood was desirable, since God placed a deep yearning for childbearing into the heart of every woman, along with the physical capacity for having children. However, the way toward fulfilling it was now marked by two fearful prospects: tremendous pain with physical changes and an altered relationship with the husband. The man's perception of his role in marriage would be tainted by the desire to control and the woman's would be tainted by a drive to manipulate or undermine. This curse would seriously affect communication. God said that the woman's "desire would be for her husband, but that he would rule over her."(v.16). Through thousands of years, Eve and all women since the Garden, have to understand this curse. When God had commanded Adam and Eve to rule over and subdue the earth, there was no hint of Adam ruling over his wife. Remember, when she was first introduced to him, he had expressed great joy and appreciation, "This is now bone of my bones and flesh of my flesh; she shall be called *woman*, for she was *taken out* of man." (Genesis 2:23) It was only when things fell apart that his emotions changed, as he struggled with his personal responsibility.

Adam's share of the fallout was equally grim. To Adam, God said:

> "Because you listened to your wife and ate from the tree about which I commanded you, 'You must not eat of it', cursed is the ground because of you; through painful toil you will eat of it all the days of your life. It will produce thorns and thistles and you will eat the plants of the field. By the sweat of your brow you will eat your food until you return to the ground, since from it you were taken; for dust you are and to dust you will return." (vs.17-19)

From now on, Adam and all other men would have to utterly busy themselves with working hard at making a living. This would preoccupy them even at the expense of a caring relationship with their families. Men would have the need to overcome God's curse, by conquering the very ground that had been given to them in pure Fatherly love. What had been given for the benefit of all, was now cursed. The *ground* would be their source of income - that farm, that business, that education, that occupation, that profession, that talent, that job – and since the curse, this *ground* has become man's identity. Being successful in a career gives modern men their illusion of being complete: intelligent, worthy, important, masculine, righteous, needed and self-fulfilled.

Why is it, however, that most wives do not confirm this identity? Having adopted career, position and status to gain self-respect and significance, men have created the image of the *self-made man*, popularized in movies and novels. It is supported by the teaching of humanistic psychology that *self-actualization* is the pinnacle of human need-fulfillment. Usually wives can see through these facades their husbands hide behind.

SUMMARY

The one and only God, who is love, created us to love and be loved. This is the hallmark of our relationship with God and subsequently between husband and wife. When God allowed this relationship to be tested, Adam and Eve walked away from their Creator. Everything that could possibly destroy that beautiful intimacy had entered creation. How kind of God to provide a way back to himself, and to one another by offering reconciliation.

Chapter Three | Assessing the Damage

"Restore us to yourself, Lord, that we may return; renew our days as of old." Lamentations 5:21

When Adam and Eve first chose the lie of Satan over the word of God, without question, the damage done to God's creation, especially to the family, was enormous. Considering that God's plan for all future generations grew out of this first family, it was inevitable that the corruption of the first family would be passed on to all the future families. Let's assess the damage in a little more detail.

Before sin entered the creation, God said about Adam: "It is not good for the man to be alone. I'll make a helper suitable for him."(Genesis 2:18) This built-in insufficiency in the man's being was developed by God, so that the man would need just the right person to complement himself. It was not a mistake, nor a faulty design. It was what God had intended from the very onset. Before that event, man was fully capable of living a fulfilling life that was pleasing to God, the Designer, and beneficial to man and to the rest of creation. However, there were two things he was not able to do: have a meaningful on-going communication with an opposite equal, and pro-create. When Eve was brought to

Adam, he somehow knew she would bring this kind of completion. For perhaps a long time[2] the two had lived and worked together in perfect harmony and respect. No wonder the devil wanted to destroy such a precious unity.

After Eden, Eve was not openly welcomed by Adam as his helper and wonderful friend any longer. Suspicion and recrimination had entered the picture. Now, Adam went so far as to accuse God of providing the wrong partner. In his distorted and deceived perception, she had become his liability. From Adam onward, all men have been busy trying to prove their adequacy, their self-sufficiency and their independence from their helper! It is not an uncommon sight, for example, to see young children playfully competing with each other. But notice the little boys trying to impress the little girls. They show off their little arm-muscles, challenge the girls to run or jump faster and brag to the girls about heroic accomplishments. Unfortunately, the little boys, about the same age as the girls, frequently lose out. Young girls are usually developmentally several years ahead of the young boys, all of which is according to God's clock. These frustrations that little boys experience at vulnerable stages invite them to resort to *mean* behavior. They like to tease, push, mock, pull hair, pinch, bite, and even beat up little girls in order to preserve some sort of self-respect, which of course leads to retaliation.

In men, since the Fall, this *broken image* has had other ramifications. Man's false sense of inadequacy and his fear of failure have opened the door to pride. In his heart he says, "I'll prove my adequacy to the world, I'll show them that I

---

[2] Adam was 130 years of age when their third son, Seth, was born (Genesis 5:3). They didn't have any children until after they were removed from the Garden (Genesis 3:23; 4:1)

am somebody." Of course, the devil greatly enjoys encouraging man's new corrupted image and offers him all kinds of remedies to overcome his apparent weakness. He holds up before men the picture of the achiever, the muscle man, the invincible guy, the man who easily conquers every woman, the military hero, the CEO who rakes in piles of money. To what avail? Has he really succeeded in convincing man of being so capable that there was no need of his God-given helper?

What effect does this have on the marriage relationship? Did God not promise to make a helper *suitable for man*? First of all, God gave the woman a strong desire to help; he also gave her insight or a special intuition, by which she could anticipate what was needed. He gave her wisdom by which she would approach her husband with suggestions of what could be done next, what would be best for the animals, what could be helpful in his work, how to improve plants, trees, birds, fish, animals and himself.

The woman's attempt to help her mate is part of God's design for her. You cannot stop a woman from being compassionate by simply refusing her help. Can you tell a mountain river to stop flowing downwards by simply putting up a dam? It will find a way around the dam and keep moving toward the valley. In the same way, a wife will find another outlet to practice helping.

The world of business has swallowed up thousands of women who were told they were *irreplaceable* or *essential* for the corporation's success. In their giftings, women are ideally suited for the corporate environment; for large or small businesses; for professions; for jobs in the entire spectrum of human enterprises. Because of their intuitive understanding of problems as well as their sociability, they keep offices, organizations, companies and politics running. Since God created them to be loyal and not easily upset by frequent changes, they bring warmth and color to the otherwise dull *work-a-day world*. The rewarding feelings women have when they are needed, cause them to enjoy working *the ground* meant for the men to work on.

****

Today's husband puts up with or even welcomes his *working wife's* diminished attention. He is satisfied with trading his relationship with his wife for the income she adds to the family budget. All too often, though, the warmth of the home will cool down considerably. Conversations become shallow. Relationships become stressed. Nobody has time or energy to discuss any issue at length any more. Serving God and his people becomes increasingly dull, a burdensome ritual. Children are encouraged to fare on their own. Family relationships get replaced with peer relationships. People become more irritable, more self-focused, less other-minded and less compassionate. Life must now be lived according to schedules. There is little room for spontaneity. Creativity reaches an all-time low because things can be easily replaced by new stuff. The modern home is no longer a training place for character and skill development, it has become a *boarding house*.

What happened to God's original plan for the family? Instead of letting God be at the center, we have allowed the world to dictate the priorities in our homes. How does King Solomon express it in Proverbs 3:5, 6? "Trust in the Lord with all your heart and lean not on your own understanding: in all your ways acknowledge him and he will direct your path."

If the ways we choose are in conflict with God's ways, then, like Adam and Eve, we simply forfeit the blessings of intimacy, security and love that marriage gives us. A principle that can be observed throughout the Bible is, that when God entrusts a responsibility to someone, he not only gives the responsibility but also the authority to execute that responsibility. The husband, who refuses to lead and recognize the authority he was given as a husband and father, opens the door to the enemy's tactics of causing disunity and distractions.

When the woman becomes a wife, through marriage to her husband, she automatically becomes his helper. She now has received the responsibility and the authority from God for her role. This means that a husband, who refuses a place for her in his life, rejecting her ways of help, resists not only his wife but God, who gave her the endowment to be his helper. How serious is that? In 1 Samuel 15:23, the Lord, speaking through Samuel to King Saul, said that rebellion (not obeying the word of God) is as the sin of witchcraft. What an indictment!

Someone may say, "Are you saying that if I don't include my wife in my business decisions, my financial affairs, my profession, my hobbies, my church, my community projects, I am going against God? If I don't discuss things with her before I make my decisions or ignore her advice in my personal life, I am rebelling against God? Do you really think I would be connecting myself to witchcraft?" What I am saying is this: just as witchcraft leads to destruction, so rebellion leads to a serious breakdown between husband and wife. Increasingly, the husband will be tempted to withhold information from his wife, screening carefully what to discuss or what to keep from her. The level of frustration for the wife, in this kind of marriage, will build up until it reaches a breaking point. The husband, on the other hand, goes about his jolly old way, interacting with all kinds of people. When he comes home from work he enjoys dinner, the computer, the TV and responds to his wife with, "Things are fine" or "Not bad" or "We had a lot to do today." Does this have anything to do with witchcraft, you ask? Simply this, somebody other than God has stepped into the marriage. Both spouses are now in the process of not satisfying each other's deepest needs of trust and intimacy. They allow other things to fill up the void. Since 'control' is a significant element in witchcraft, it becomes necessary to examine who is taking control of the marriage.

SUMMARY

The loss of intimacy with God from Adam's time has caused the human race to become independent and self-centered. Man's search for significance and security has become a very costly pursuit. How can we fill the emptiness of our souls when we turn away from God? All that the *prince of the air* offers to a married couple is external and keeps us craving for more. This lust drives us further away from God and one another.

Chapter Four | Cleaving or Leaving

"The Lord our God is merciful and forgiving, even though we have rebelled against him ..." Daniel 9:9

The following story of Glenn and Erica could represent thousands of couples who have gone down this road. It could be your story.

Glenn grew up in a home of six children - he was the second youngest. His father was a heavy drinker whose goal seemed to be to turn his kids into vicious creatures like himself. He would mock them, belittle them, rage at them, beat them, and drive them to the point of despair. Glenn fought his way through school and beat up the boys who disrespected him. He was bright and talented, but unable to sit still long enough to benefit from school. Inside, he felt the growing emptiness of failure and loss. He yearned to be loved and accepted.

At age seventeen, he met Erica, a cute girl who treated him kindly and managed to ignore his rough behavior. She stood by him and defended him when others would egg him on. Erica came from a Christian home that had good morals. Her influence on Glenn was remarkable. Within a year, Glenn surrendered his life to Jesus. Both started to think of a future together. Deep inside, Glenn was very insecure. He was stereotypically a guy who had missed out on a father's love and affirmation. He tried to overcome his haunting insecurity by pressurizing Erica to have premarital sex. This really upset her. Her goals were to please her Lord Jesus Christ, to whom she had committed her life. She stood on abstinence. She wanted to graduate from high school and be a missionary. However, Glenn's pressure increased. He desperately needed to prove that he was in control. He accused her of not loving him, nor caring for his needs and finally Glenn threatened to walk away. At that point, Erica gave in. As a result, her worst fears came true -- she got pregnant! They were trapped. They felt too young for marriage. After much arguing, however, they both agreed against abortion and with the help of her family, they made hasty plans to get married.

****

Over the following four years, they had two more children. They tried to be good parents and love their three little ones. A job promotion moved them from the mid-west to the west coast of the United States. Erica got pregnant again in the seventh year of their marriage. Somehow her dream of serving as missionaries together was slipping away. She started to suffer from deep feelings of guilt. She realized that she had gone back on her promise to God. Glenn had tried hard to get into a higher pay scale in the company, but nothing seemed to work for him. Erica tried to help Glenn by teaching him better computer skills, to keep him up-to-date, but he openly resisted her *meddling*. He couldn't handle the pressure of supporting a growing family, dealing with the requirements of his company and living so far away from close friends and relatives. He began to lose what he had learned about God, and started to drink, which he had vowed never to do. Glenn saw his wife's genuine concern as constant nagging. He questioned her commitment to him, because she was still looking beautiful, even after four children. He was losing hair. Inwardly, he was plagued with jealousy whenever they went to social events. At work, he started to confide in a younger woman about his marriage. Reluctant to stray, however, Glenn began visiting pornographic sites on the internet.

Erica had no clue about this new intrusive barrier. She had already distanced herself from Glenn with a deep sadness she could not explain. To make herself be jolted out of her depression, Erica eventually decided to take up a job a friend had offered her. It would bring in more money to support the family, pay the bills, and give her a chance to learn new things.

Soon Erica was enjoying the attention she got at her job and although they had been married for twelve years, Erica was contemplating divorce. There seemed to be no end to their constant fighting. Glenn's increased drinking brought about a meanness towards the children that had begun to trouble her. Her job was also wearing her down physically, but she had made up her mind never to mention it. A friend of Erica's suggested she put the divorce plans on hold and go to a Biblical counselor first, to see if he might help them solve the problems. Reluctantly, Glenn agreed to give *counseling* a try.

****

Over the following months, the counselor helped Glenn give up his drinking as well as his porn habits. This was a major accomplishment. Glenn also recognized that because

45

of his own sense of failure, inferiority and worthlessness he had rejected his wife and all her attempts to help him. Drinking and pornography had given a false and short-lived boost to his self-inflicted damage on his masculinity. He had related to the images on the screen as though they were in the room with him. They seemed to understand his needs without requiring changes. One day, falling on his knees before God and his wife, Glenn sobbed out his terrible regrets to Erica. He asked her forgiveness for having closed himself off from her. Erica was unable to forgive Glenn at first. She had felt *abused* from the time before the marriage. But with the help of the counselor, Erica learned to forgive herself and, in time, her husband. She acknowledged her great disappointment to God, asking Him for his forgiveness for her backslidden years. As Erica opened up to receive God's love afresh, she found a renewed capacity for helping Glenn with his last step. Glenn was working hard to be able to forgive his father for all the evil he had brought into their family when he was growing up.

Restoring the cut-off relationship with his dad gave Glenn the strength to overcome the self-hatred he had battled most of his life. Because he knew that God had forgiven him, he was able to forgive his father for not having been there for the kids, for having beaten his mother and for having cheated on her. Finally, Glenn was willing to release his dad from the many insults he had heaped on him. One day, Glenn even phoned his dad to tell him that he loved him, something he had never done. His dad was totally caught off guard and started to cry. It was a victory over rejection and failure.

Glenn learned from his mother that his grandfather had been very much like his dad. He could see how sins were passed on from one generation to the next. Glenn and Erica prayed with the counselor against other curses that had been passed down. By faith, they cut the evil ties from previous generations. They learned that they could pray these prayers because of Jesus' work on the cross. They claimed the freedom that Christ had already won on their behalf (Galatians 3:13) for their immediate and future families.

Another step that had a profound effect on his family happened when Glenn sat down with each child to ask forgiveness for having been *so mean*. He asked them to forgive him for his drinking and for not having spent more time with them. They all forgave him. In turn, they asked him for forgiveness for not having liked him during those years. As the family made these major changes, they pulled together and eventually saw the results they had long hoped for.

****

The devil is as relentless in his attacks as an insect or weed is relentless. Therefore, we are cautioned to be alert and to pray. Our enemy prowls around like a roaring lion, seeking to devour us. The apostle Peter instructs us to resist him and to stand firm in our faith. (1 Peter 5:6-9) Through the counseling, Glenn and Erica learned to use the spiritual weapons offered to Christians, especially the weapons of prayer and the Word of God. They gained new confidence in hearing God's voice and making wise decisions. One of those decisions was based on an insight Glenn received during his morning devotional time. He was reading 2 Corinthians 9:6, 7, "But this I say: He who sows sparingly will also reap sparingly, and he who sows bountifully will also reap bountifully, for God loves a cheerful giver." Glenn shared this with Erica and as they discussed what Glenn had received, they decided to become *cheerful givers*. True to God's word, God blessed them financially; Glenn finally got the raise he had asked for. However, after much prayer by family and friends, Glenn decided to go into business by himself. When it was up and running, Erica quit her job to work with her husband. Glenn was no longer threatened by his wife's input. Erica felt free to work at home or at the business place. Accepted and appreciated by her husband, Erica could step out into the community and lead in areas unfamiliar to her. Glenn and Erica supported each other when their four children became teenagers. Today, they are involved in counseling other troubled marriages.

The story of Glenn and Erica is a familiar one. Too many couples opt for a divorce, leaving deep emotional wounds for all involved, particularly the children. To help couples caught up in this battle, it is good to take a longer look into how conflicts develop. What can we, as Christians, do to prevent or resolve them? In Ephesians 6:12 we read:

> "For we are not fighting against people made of flesh and blood, but against persons without bodies—the evil rulers of the unseen world, those mighty satanic beings and great evil princes of darkness who rule this world; and against huge numbers of wicked spirits in the spirit world." (Eph. 6:12, TLB)

In the next chapter we will explore a strategy that "evil rulers" and "wicked spirits," use to cause havoc in families. We will study what can be done about such strategies.

SUMMARY

Having lost intimacy with God through sin inevitably leads us to make choices that ruin a person's life and the lives of our immediate and extended family. Not until we humble ourselves and take responsibility for our choices, can the road to recovery begin and relationships be restored. Repentance from sins we have committed, and forgiveness to those that were committed against us, is God's provision for healing and reconciliation.

Chapter Five | Strongholds to Demolish

"You will keep him in perfect peace whose mind is stayed on You, because he trusts in You." Isaiah 26:3 (NKJV)

The enemy mostly uses a two-pronged approach to destroy marriages and families: fear and lies. Satan knows that the most effective period in people's lives to be attacked is during childhood. So he causes the damage that can set them up for failure later in life by inducing fear and planting lies about their true identity during early years. How does he do it? Through intimidation, shouting, belittling, inappropriate punishment, being forced to watch scary movies, the heart of a child is filled with threatening images and emotions.

The most vulnerable and impressionable years in the child's development are between two and six. Although a child's language has developed quite adequately for general communication, the complex process of reasoning and understanding, needed to grasp many of the verbal commands people in *authority* throw at the child, are beyond them. Their cognitive developmental stage cannot make logical sense of what people demand of them. Authority figures, like parents, older siblings, and extended family members, are often perceived as threatening, inside a child's immature mind. They generally assume what is said must be true because the people are bigger and louder than them. The child accepts their words without questioning because it has no comparisons.

At that age he or she perceives language in images and emotions rather than cognitively. Consequently, destructive words expressed in a harsh tone of voice, accompanied by threatening gestures are deeply embedded in the child's memory. These early images form negative strongholds that serve as the main influencers of a boy or girl's growing up years. These strongholds determine the choices people make during their life-time, such as the kind of friends they prefer, the kind of social activities they engage in, even the kind of career they chose.

Psychiatrist Erik Erikson has come up with eight psychosocial stages that people move through from birth to death.[3] Each stage in Erikson's theory is concerned with becoming skilled in an area of life. If the stage is handled well, the person will feel a sense of mastery. If the stage is managed poorly, the person will emerge with a sense of inadequacy. Erikson believed that at each stage, people experience a crisis which serves as a turning point in their development. In Erikson's view, these conflicts are centered on either developing a psychological competence or failing to develop that competence. During these times, the potential for personal growth is high, but so is the potential for failure.

The first stage Erikson calls *Trust vs. Mistrust* which extends from birth to age one. An infant learns trust when his

---

[3] Erikson, Erik H. (1959) *Identity and the Life Cycle.* New York: International Universities Press.

basic needs are met and mistrust when the child is left crying for extended periods of time before attention is given to his needs of food and comfort.

Erikson calls the second stage *Autonomy vs. Shame and Doubt*. Considering the enormous amount of learning the toddler, age one to three, has to master, the child needs to receive much assurance that he can do it by him or herself, particularly in the area of toilet training, motor coordination skills and language development. It is easy to discourage the little one by too much control, creating shame and doubt that the he will ever succeed. Subsequent stages, like Stage 3, *Initiative vs. Guilt* (Preschool age three to six years) and Stage 4, *Industry vs. Inferiority* (School-age six to eleven), are equally crucial in fostering confidence to approach increased challenges. Failure to move through these stages with a growing boldness and self-reliance can result in psychosocial maladaptation and growing self-doubt. It may cause the person to resort to destructive behavior in order to cope with a growing sense of inferiority and inadequacy.

In Glenn's case, it is quite evident, that because of an unfair share of harsh treatment during his earliest years, he adopted aggression as his control over others. This served as a cover up for the fear of being rejected and labeled inadequate. He demanded respect by beating up other kids -- intimidating them as he had been intimidated by his dad. When he met Erica he gladly responded to her unconditional acceptance. And after he had become a Christian, he still operated out of his deep-seeded fear. His need to dominate Erica in the structure that gave him security was done, not by beating her up, but by subjugating her sexually. He needed her to see him as superior and in charge. That was the manner in which they had lived for most of their marriage.

How did the enemy manage to re-introduce these destructive forces, thousands of years after Genesis? We saw in Chapter Two, that when Satan attacked the family and Adam and Eve fell for his lies, God spelled out the consequences of their disobedience (Genesis 3:16). The Lord told Eve, "Your desire will be for your husband, but he will rule over you." Why, I often ask myself, do men even have that need to rule over their wives? My wife and I have worked in numerous countries – both developed and developing nations – and we have seen this pattern everywhere, regardless of education or affluence. The extent of the need for domination and control that men exercise over their wives is really quite frightening. It should be of great alarm to us as Christians. I can only trace this male tendency back to Adam when he recognized his nakedness, his transparency and his separation from God. For the first time, Adam experienced total aloneness, along with a deep sense of failure and worthlessness.

When Eve desired her husband, he understood that she loved him. But it was not the kind of love that could replace what they had lost. Because of separation from God, who IS love (1. John 4:16), mankind is on the continual search for love. The man thinks that by controlling the one who desires him, he possesses her. Not controlling her would mean losing what was his by nature. Therefore, when the person he controls shows signs of independence, he understands it as danger. In the heart of the man, independence on the part of the woman provokes that feeling of total aloneness and abandonment. One solution for him is extending even more control, involving force if necessary. This kind of control, which is called domestic violence, is all too prevalent in every nation. It is the source of untold grief and suffering for married women.

So what was it that finally destroyed the influential, negative stronghold in Glenn's mind? Let us look at 2. Corinthians 10:3-5. Here the LORD, through the Apostle Paul says the following:

> "For though we live in the world, we do not wage war as the world does. The weapons we fight with are not the weapons of the world. On the contrary, they have divine power to demolish strongholds. We demolish arguments and every pretension that sets itself up against the knowledge of God, and we take captive every thought to make it obedient to Christ."

Paul explains that the strongholds needing demolishing are "arguments and pretensions that set themselves up against the true knowledge of God." In other Bible translations these are called *vain imaginations* or *lofty thoughts (AMP)*. Notice here the strong language Paul uses: *strongholds, demolish, take captive*. These are terms used to describe military operations. He also mentions that our weapons are powerful only through God. In other words, they are the weapons made available to disciples of Jesus. His finished work on the cross gives believers his armory. Nevertheless, the place where they are to be used is *in this world*. It is quite clear that the mind is the battlefield where early childhood strongholds wage their war. Our will, our memories, our thought-life become the theatre of operations. All strongholds referred to in this passage, whether reasonable, intellectual, or fanciful are ideas against the true knowledge of God. Much of what is in schools, colleges, and universities comes under this category of strongholds. For example, the fanatical push to teach evolution, certain destructive philosophies, like existential philosophy, secular humanism, or a-moral ethics, often build on the strongholds already present in our young minds. As a result they form a grid through which our youth screen new information. Ideas formed in addition to old strongholds subsequently become the framework for evaluating themselves and the world around them.

In Glenn's situation, the deep stronghold of self-rejection had come mostly via his father's verbal abuse. Once that was clear to him, Glenn got an insight of Satan's work in his life. He realized that God would have never said the things about him that his earthly father had told him, "You're just so stupid"; "Nobody gives a hoot about you"; "You'll never amount to anything". As he studied Psalm 139, the Holy Spirit opened Glenn's mind to the truth about himself: that he was precious, that he had been tenderly formed in his mother's womb and that God had numbered every day of his life. The Lord was allowed to bring healing to his soul. A deep peace came over Glenn. He asked God for forgiveness in blaming so many people for the things that had gone wrong in his life. He told God he would take responsibility for his own actions. For the first time in his life, he could really understand what Jesus had accomplished, when Christ paid the price for his sins. As he forgave his father, the stronghold of self-rejection and worthlessness finally lost its grip on Glenn. He opened his heart to receive the love of his heavenly Father. During the times of counseling, other strongholds were identified. Some were: *I will never depend on anybody because I can't trust anybody*; or *I have to be strong*; or *There is nobody who understands me*; *Men don't show their emotions.* By identifying these strongholds, they could be denounced (or demolished, as the Bible says). Their (false) authority was cancelled by the blood of Jesus. In this way, the old thought processes lost their effectiveness.

Glenn walked through the whole area of resentments. Some people in his life had become strong *authorities* to him.[4] These illegitimate authorities had blocked the loving authority of his heavenly Father from guiding his life. Some of the people that he forgave were already dead. Yet, their actions and the memories of what they had done or said kept stirring up deep emotions and memories. This often left him with a sense of helplessness. He wanted to lash out at them, but they were no longer around. So, he would direct his hostility towards people who were around, especially those closest to him. When he saw how he had misplaced his own resentments by making his wife and children suffer, he couldn't stop weeping.

Finally, the authorities from the past lost their ability to harass him with anger, resentment and self-hatred, as he forgave each one. Erica received a whole new husband. Freedom had come into Glenn's heart. He was not afraid to be helped by his wife. In fact, the opposite was true. Now he would ask her for her input. God gave them a new love for each other. Erica's trust in her husband soared. She saw his eagerness to read the Bible. When Glenn was eventually asked to teach an adult Sunday Bible Study class at their church, Erica could only marvel at how God had turned him and their marriage around. It was better now than either one had ever imagined.

---

[4] Jesus taught his disciples in Matthew 6:24 "No one can serve two masters; for either he will hate the one and love the other, or else he will be loyal to the one and despise the other." We cannot let the voices of the past rule over us any longer. They have lost their authority to dictate to us at the very moment we surrender to the lordship of Jesus Christ.

SUMMARY

Strongholds are powerful thoughts in our mind that have been planted there over the years of our life. They are usually the opposite of what God, our Father, would call us. Whom do we believe? We break the power of such strongholds by forgiving those who spoke them to us, and forgiving ourselves and repenting for having bought into such lies. We are called to demolish such strongholds. We have the ability to take every thought captive and make it obedient to Christ. (2 Corinthians 10:3-5) The battle is fought over our mind, but we have been given the authority to keep undesirable powers from using it.

Chapter Six | The Weapons of Our Warfare

"The weapons we fight with are not the weapons of the world. On the contrary, they have divine power ..." 2 Corinthians 10:3-5

The prospect of prolonged warfare is not a very encouraging one, as we have learned anew these past decades. As part of the human race, we have long known that we have an adversary. The fact is that Christians are under constant attack. Some attacks are merely emotional or spiritual harassment, probably designed to wear us down. Some days our feelings are up, a few days later we struggle to get to work. Other attacks are *temptations*: lies that lead to wrong ideas, which lead to wrong actions, which lead to tragic consequences, like eating the fruit in Eden. Every day we hear of tragedies people inflict on each other and wonder how they could happen. The Bible clearly states that the believer has an enemy who goes about as a *roaring lion*.[5] As the military in this spiritual war, we need to know about our enemy, his goals and strategies. The Apostle Paul writes, "For we are not unaware of his (Satan's) schemes..." (2 Corinthians 2:11)

---

[5] 1 Peter 5:8 Be alert and of sober mind. Your enemy the devil prowls around like a roaring lion looking for someone to devour.

Satan's goal has been to eliminate competition to his self-proclaimed rulership, as declared in Isaiah 14:14, "I will make myself like the Most High." He sees the human race as his target. What he is afraid of, are the people who have surrendered to Jesus Christ. When they do that, they begin to work in harmony with God's plans for marriages and families. Therefore, a primary target of the devil is to destroy the family. He aims at the marriage relationship first, and then attacks the children as young as possible.

How does Satan accomplish that? Mostly he uses a relentless bombardment of our minds with wrong thoughts, distorted memories, prejudice, suspicions, and outright lies about people, events or situations, judgmental and critical assumptions. He initiates wedges between sexes, family members, generations, business partners, leaders and followers.

In order to thwart Satan's efforts, we have been issued superior weaponry along with superior authority and a superior objective. This objective is spelled out in the Lord's Prayer, "Your Kingdom come; your will be done, on earth as it is in Heaven."(Matthew 6:10-13) Our superior authority stems from our relationship with our Lord who says of Himself, 'ALL authority in heaven and on earth has been given to me' (Matthew 28:18). In Mark 16:17,18 Jesus says, "In my name they will drive out demons; they will speak in new tongues; they will pick up snakes with their hands; and when they drink deadly poison, it will not hurt them at all; they will place their hands on sick people, and they will get well."

We can see that the first weapon of our warfare is belonging to Jesus Christ. He gives us the right to use his name against the works of the enemy. In the name of Jesus, we can command demons to flee, sicknesses to be gone and evil situations to depart from us. My wife used to suffer from severe migraine headaches, which would come in waves that lasted two to four days. No medication could bring her relief! A friend had reminded us of my authority in Christ, as a husband, to lay hands on Elsie and pray. One night as she was pacing upstairs and downstairs, with righteous anger and determination, I put my hands on her head and ordered the migraine to get out of my wife. I must admit that this approach was very new to us. To our great surprise, in an instant she was pain free and went upstairs to sleep peacefully throughout the night! From that day on, she has stopped having those wretched headaches.

The next weapon we have as believers is the Word of God. As our friend Dr. Glenn Martin frequently mentioned in his lectures, the Bible comes to us as truth in *verbal propositional* terms.[6] It comes as light to disperse all darkness; it illumines the motives of the heart and drives untruths from our minds. In the Biblical mindset, truth is not merely a concept or a philosophical statement. Truth is a person. Truth is Jesus Christ who says of himself, "I am the way, the truth and the life" in John 14:6. Therefore, when we speak the Word of God against the powers of Satan, we are standing with Jesus against the devil and we are quoting from the document that establishes our identity. We are not insignificant, nameless, easily victimized persons. We stand against lies and the father of lies with the person of truth and honesty. Quoting Scripture right to Satan's face drives him away. Quoting Scripture establishes a truthful take on reality, records our jurisdictional authority and describes how to use

---

[6] Dr. Glenn Martin is the late professor of History and Social Sciences at Indiana Wesleyan University in Marion, Indiana.

our arsenal. Remember, when Jesus was tempted by the devil in the wilderness (Luke 4:1-13), every temptation hurled at Jesus was defeated with a verse from the Old Testament?. Do we need to know and memorize scripture verses? Of course. How can we possibly use this weapon effectively without knowing how to quote the Bible easily?

Another mighty, state of the art weapon is prayer. Jesus scolded his sleepy disciples in the garden, "Why are you sleeping? Get up and pray so that you will not fall into temptation."(Luke 22:46) Paul asked the Christians in Ephesus to:

> "...pray in the Spirit on all occasions with all kinds of prayers and requests. With this in mind, be alert and always keep on praying for all the saints. Pray also for me, that whenever I open my mouth, words may be given me so that I will fearlessly make known the mystery of the gospel. Pray that I may declare it fearlessly, as I should." (Ephesians 6:18-20)

Paul was absolutely convinced of the power of prayer. The words *prayer*, *pray* or *prayed* is mentioned in his letters over one hundred and thirty times. He certainly defeated the enemy through effectual prayers. So must we.

Along with this important weapon, is the weapon of fasting. In Acts 9:9 we read that "for three days he (Paul) was blind, and did not eat or drink anything." Again, in Acts 14:23, "Paul and Barnabas appointed elders in each church and, with prayer and fasting, committed them to the Lord in whom they had put their trust." Jesus told us that in difficult situations, both prayer and fasting are needed. (Mark 9:29)

Two other essential weapons in our arsenal set are repentance and forgiveness. Satan's effectiveness in people's lives is based on the open doors that sin offers him. Heartfelt repentance from sin, when the blood of Jesus has really been applied, firmly closes the door through which the devil attacks and limits his effectiveness in us.

If the devil can't torture us over our own sins, he loves to plant roots of bitterness in us over the sins of others. These roots of bitterness are no laughing matter. The older we get, the harder it is to get these roots out of us. They tend to become like an addiction. Many a personality has been warped and twisted, and turned dark and ugly by them. The writer to the Hebrews warns us in Hebrews 12:15 (NKJV), "looking carefully lest anyone fall short of the grace of God; lest any root of bitterness springing up cause trouble, and by this many become defiled;". By forgiving freely we not only protect our own hearts from bitterness, but we hamper the enemy's work in the lives of others.

SUMMARY

Satan has instructed his army of demons to plant every conceivable lie into people's mind that would make them think too highly or too little of themselves. This strategy is intended to cause struggles in marriages and families, where the husband, the wife, or the children continuously feel like failures, and struggle with rejection and inferiority. God has given us vastly superior weapons that have divine power to demolish such crippling thoughts and feelings. Some of these weapons are: the Word of God, which always speaks truth about us; prayer and fasting; and repentance and forgiveness.

Chapter Seven | Becoming One

"For I know the plans I have for you,' declares the Lord, 'Plans to prosper you and not to harm you, plans to give you hope and a future.'"
Jeremiah 29:11

Have you ever noticed that God didn't create Adam and Eve to laze around in his garden? No, from the beginning he gave them things to do. In fact, he created the first job descriptions. He kept them brief, so that neither of them could say, *"Oh, sorry. I didn't have time to read all the pages."* To Adam, God said, "Keep the garden and care for it." God made Eve to be the only helper to Adam in doing that work. So we see from the outset that God created people with a purpose. What was true for Adam and Eve is true for every person since then. God intends us to fulfill the mandates of being productive in the areas assigned to us, in accordance to our abilities and callings. The apostle Paul writes in Romans 11:29, that "the gifts and the calling are irrevocable." At what point do we receive the call? Is the call or the purpose of our life fixed before we were born, and therefore difficult to find or do we realize it at some point during our lifetime? God spoke to Jeremiah about the nation of Israel in Jeremiah 29:11 "'For I know the plans I have for you' declares the Lord, 'plans to prosper you and not to harm you, plans to give you hope and a future.'" We can assume that the God who makes plans for a nation, makes plans for an individual as well. In the first chapter of Jeremiah, God tells the young prophet, "Before I formed you in the womb I knew you, before you were born I set you apart; I appointed you as a prophet to the nations." (verse 5). And in Isaiah 49:1 and 5 we read, "before I was born the Lord called me; from birth he has made mention of my name...he who formed me in the womb to be his servant..."

There is no question that God is the holder of the plan for our lives. He sets the plan in motion even before we are born. Remember the story of Moses. Even the decree of Pharaoh to kill all the Israelite male children, of whom Moses was one, did not prevent Moses from fulfilling his God-given destiny. In another account, we find the lovely Esther entering a beauty contest at a time when the Jewish population was in danger of being annihilated. The King, who married Esther, listened to his wife (pretty smart guy!), and destroyed the plan of the evil Haman. (Esther 2-5) Esther's life in the palace was God's plan to save the Jewish citizens in Xerxes' empire. Her cousin and mentor, Mordecai, recognized God's hand in all of the happenings and said, "And who knows but that you have come to royal position for such a time as this?" (Esther 4:14)

Does God have a plan for everybody who was and will be born? Personally, I believe he does, for it says that he loves the whole world (John 3:16) and that he is without partiality. In Deuteronomy 10:17, it says, "For the LORD your God is God of gods and Lord of lords, the great God, mighty and awesome, who shows no partiality and accepts no bribes." Every person has the desire to be significant and contribute something to the world during his or her lifetime, but will everybody enter into his or her calling? And here I must say that *many people will not*. Why? Because we were created to be unique with a free will. God includes each of us in the quest of finding his purpose for our lives. He says to Israel in Jeremiah 33:3, "Call on me and I will show you great and mighty things which you don't know yet." Finding God's will for a nation, a family, a couple or an individual can be both exciting and arduous. But God is a Person who loves to communicate with us. The Bible says that we as God's sheep "know his voice." (John 10:4) That brings up the age old question, "How does he tell us his plans? How do we hear from God?[7] This question has fascinated modern man a great deal. More books have been written on the topic of hearing God's voice in the last half century than in all human history. In his book *Is That Really You God?*, Loren Cunningham, the founder of the modern world's largest Evangelical Christian missions movement, says,

> "Hearing God is not all that difficult. If we know the Lord, we have already heard His voice - after all it was the inner leading that brought us to Him in the first place. But we can hear His voice and still miss His best if we don't keep on listening. After the *what* of guidance comes the *when* and *how*. Jesus always checked with His Father (John 8:26-29) and so should

---

[7] I would like to refer you to a couple of excellent books on this subject as supplementary reading. The one is *'Intimacy with God'*, by the excellent Bible teacher Joy Dawson, and the other book, *'Is That Really You God'* by Loren Cunningham, founder of Youth With A Mission (YWAM (Both books are available in most Christian bookstores or over the Internet).

we; hearing the voice of the heavenly Father is a basic right of every child of God."[8]

For somebody to approach God with a sincere heart and ask, "Lord, show me the purpose for my life" or "Lord, what would you have me become?", "How can I prepare for that?" - God will answer you, perhaps not all at once, but you will hear God's voice. He may confirm the answer in different ways: through another person, through a prophecy, through circumstances, through an *open door*, through your parents or teachers, through people who have noticed your skills or talents. Usually God's calling is related to something that you have cherished for a long time. In Psalm 37:4 you are encouraged to "delight yourself in the LORD and he will give you the desires of your heart."

God may ask you to change location, change your approach, research the area, join others, or go for special training. For the fishermen who became Jesus' disciples, it meant leaving their fishing business and learning how to *fish* for people. For Moses, it meant re-purposing his shepherd's rod. For young David, it meant using the fighting skills he had learned in the Judean hills.

One of the tragedies of the civilized world is the number of people who wander aimlessly through their lives, alienated, unhappy and unfulfilled. Modern marriages suffer when the husband and father has no clear goal for his life or when the wife and mother doubts the eternal significance of her role. Children from such homes frequently fall into a similar pattern of doubting themselves. They are indecisive about their future. Why should addicts surrender their destructive

---

[8] *Is That Really You, God?:* Hearing the Voice of God. Seattle, WA: YWAM Publishing, 2001. pp 161-2

ways, when they have no purpose for living? Why should an older couple stop watching TV all day long when they feel they are no longer useful?

As a counselor for a Juvenile and Family Court in Canada, I worked with delinquent youths for a number of years. My experience taught me that no amount of counseling will avail unless one can direct the young person to do something that gives him purpose. In most cases, the reason they started their delinquent activities in the first place was to get some sense of significance. Delinquency provided them attention from their family and community.

In the case of married couples, the oneness God promised them when he said, "the two will become one flesh"[9] flows naturally from a purposeful life together. The two are drawn closer over time by the strength of shared memories, shared goals and shared efforts. One thing my wife and I have noticed about couples is this: marriages that focus exclusively inward grow dull very quickly; marriages that have godly goals outside of themselves develop an incredible capacity to overcome life's conflicts and sudden adversities with an unshakeable calm. Together, they follow the plan that God intended for their lives.

How do we find God's plan for our own marriage or family? This depends on the phase of life you are currently in. Are you are newlywed couple? Have you been married for many years? Are you a family already? Do you feel you are at a crossroad in your life? Are you a new Christian, asking God what you should do with the rest of your life? Or maybe you are wondering whether God is pleased with the way you have lived in your marriage and family? You see, it is good to take

---

[9] Genesis 2:24 (NKJV)

inventory periodically and ask God how He sees your marriage. Have you neglected times of praying together, reading and studying the Bible together? Have you let the word of God speak to you as a family? If not, you can always start anew with a time of repentance. Many Christians argue that God gave us a mind of our own with which to make decisions, so why should we go to God with every little thing? In response, I say, "Thank God for having given us a sound mind with which to think. But the question is, "Who and what influences our thinking?" The Apostle Paul wrote to the church in Rome, "Do not conform to the pattern of this world, but be transformed by the renewing of your mind. Then, you will be able to test and approve what God's will is—his good, pleasing and perfect will." (Romans 12:2)

God's desire for our lives is out of his character of love and goodness. He delights to see us fulfilled in what we are doing. Remember His words, "For I know the plans I have for you," declares the Lord, "plans to prosper you and not to harm you, plans to give you hope and a future. (Jeremiah 29:11).

SUMARRY

The unity we so desire in marriage when we stand at the altar before God with our *I do's* encompasses our entire life. We are to become *one flesh*, in the physical, emotional, intellectual, and spiritual ways, but we are to be one in our work together, in raising our children together – in seeking God's plan for the future. *Becoming one* involves every area of our lives as a married couple and family.

Chapter Eight | Train Up Your Child

"Train up a child in the way he should go and when he is old he will not depart from it." Proverbs 22:6

It sounds very simple, doesn't it? Having observed families for decades, we wonder whether parents give sufficient thought in training their children. What is it they actually want their children to learn? What would parents have their children become? Which goals do they keep in mind while raising their children? What would the parents themselves like to accomplish? What is the vision for their family? Are their children simply to drift inevitably from cute, cuddly little angels, to independent adults? What do parents *feed their children* for spiritual and emotional growth? How much thought goes into developing their character?

A few weeks ago my wife and I watched a talk show that featured a group of mothers whose topic of discussion was, "Do children help or hinder the happiness of your marriage?" We were perturbed at both the topic and comments. The general consensus was that children add significant stress to the relationship between husband and wife. Several of the women actually wished they had never had children. Only one in four were enjoying their children amid the normal marital struggles.

Why is this perception out there that marriage is mainly for the purpose of individual gratification? When did children become a nuisance instead of a blessing? This thinking is so contrary to God's intentions. One of the first things God told Adam and Eve was to *multiply*. Psalm 127:3-5 says that "sons are a heritage from the Lord, children a reward from him. Blessed is the man whose quiver is full of them. They will not be put to shame when they contend with their enemies in the gate." How far we have drifted from that Biblical view! It seems we've forgotten that being a parent is an amazing privilege!

Children cannot be put on *auto-training* like a pilot putting the plane on *auto-landing*. Children do not train themselves *in the way they should go*. The command to the parents is to *train up a child in the way he should go*. To do this takes time, knowledge, practice and commitment.

Let's look at what is involved in training a child. The following are three basic, necessary phases in doing training. The first is *instruction*, the second is *practice*, and the third is *discipline*. They are logically in that order. Let's see why.

****

If you are old enough to read this book, you'll know that the clearer the instructions, the better the performance. To be effective, instruction should be at the same maturity level as the person to be instructed. Parents who are training their children can begin the instruction phase with a few simple and basic methods. They may assure understanding by use of repetition. For example, you may have heard the frequently-told story about Vince Lombardi taking over as coach of the

National Football League's Green Bay Packers. At their first practice, wanting to teach them from the foundation upwards, he took a football and threw it to one of the players. "What are you holding in your hand?" he asked. Now, in football you can't start more basic than that. Give only easy teaching for the first practice session. Parents need to give one rule at a time and allow for repeated opportunities to practice before giving the next rule to focus on. Remember, the rules are to lead to *the way the child should go*. That *way* is based on Biblical truth and not arbitrary, ambitious, subjective wish lists parents may have. The end result of this whole instructing program is to help the child to grow to another level of maturity. In Hebrews 5:14 we read, "But solid food is for the mature, who by constant use have trained themselves to distinguish (discern) good from evil." Solid food refers to a person's steady diet of sound Bible study and meditation. The *good* to be recognized and practiced is not something that is good because the majority of people approve it, but because it is based on Biblical truth. It requires daily exercising of right over wrong in simple steps.

****

There is a saying that "repetition is the mother of learning." Repetition is definitely needed after the child has been shown and has been given the chance to try it by himself. A toddler, who is expected to pick up his or her toys after playing with them, needs to be told (and shown) exactly how it should be done. For the first few times after the instructions, the parent should lead by example, doing it together and pick them up with the child, gradually letting the toddler take the lead. Remember modeling. Modeling can take place in the parent's bedroom, the kitchen, the garage, the car and the parent's desks, inviting participation while pointing out that daddy and mommy are putting their things away after using them, too. This collaborative effort between parent and child was an area of interest for the Russian psychologist, Lev Vygotsky. He was born in the U.S.S.R. in 1896, and is responsible for the *Social Development Theory of Learning*. He proposed that social interaction profoundly influences cognitive development. Central to Vygotsky's theory is his belief that biological and cultural development do not occur in isolation (Driscoll, 1994). He proposed that a young person can perform a task under adult or peer guidance that could not be achieved alone. Vygotsky calls it the *Zone of Proximal Development* and describes it as "the distance between the actual development level, which is determined by independent problem solving, and the level of potential development, as determined through problem solving under adult guidance." Collaboration with more capable peers bridges that gap between what is known and what can be known. Vygotsky claimed that much learning occurs in this zone.

****

The third stage of training means consistency in spite of circumstances. Discipline includes recognizing the consequences of choices. What is right today is also right tomorrow, or in a week from tomorrow; in a public place, or at home; when the parent is tired or when everyone is at ease. If the child is clear about certain consequences for disobedience, the relationship between parent and child will be less stressful. Both parents need to be involved in disciplining. However, the administration of the more serious kind, like spanking, should be handled as much as possible by the father. This frees the mother to be more involved in her role as nurturer and comforter.

During my time as a counselor in the Juvenile and Family Courts in Canada, I observed how the judges had a list of the various measures of disciplines at their disposal. Repeat offenders appearing before the judge, for example, had to be given increasingly harsher forms of punishments compared to those who had no prior records in court. In the same way, it may be a good idea for parents to agree on making a list of disciplines that should be used for certain offenses. When an incidence occurs, the parent already knows ahead of time of how to respond. Believe me, incidences will occur. One family we observed over longer periods of time, made very effective use of *time-outs*, simply by sending the child to a designated corner for a few minutes. Even at age two, the child was able to change her behavior. Time-outs can be effective for toddlers and very young children.

Another form of discipline with proven effects in later childhood, is removing privileges, such as no playtime for two days; no tablet or TV watching for a week; no friends over for a week; or other meaningful suspensions. For teens this might mean additional chores to be done, no keys to the car for a week; no meeting with close friends; no mobile phone; no allowance money; and other such restrictions. The time limits need to be reasonable, yet severe enough to emphasize that disobedience has consequences. Most of this kind of disciplining needs to be done by the mother, who normally spends more time with the children at home. However, the husband must back up his wife, so that her word is as good as his (or vice versa).

Generally speaking, the Bible indicates that disciplining is the father's responsibility. "Moreover, we have all had human

fathers who disciplined us and we respected them for it."
(Hebrews 12:9) Keep in mind that disagreements on how to
handle certain situations have to be resolved by the parents in
private. Children become confused when parents argue, in
front of them, as to how they should be disciplined. They will
quickly learn to take advantage of one parent's leniency and
will attempt to split parental authority. Inevitably, this teaches
the child the art of manipulation.

Some of you may wonder whether physical punishment
is appropriate or even necessary. Since the early 1970s, this
topic was the subject of much controversy. At that time, I
was working in a Child Guidance Clinic in Canada and
remember the seminars we had to attend with endless staff
discussions. The question was, "What constitutes child abuse?
Is spanking child abuse?" In the years following, legislation
was introduced that resulted in parents being put in jail
because somebody had reported them for spanking their
child. Neighbors or witnesses were required to report them or
else they themselves would become equally guilty of child
abuse. It was very unfortunate that spanking became
synonymous with child abuse. Even today the subject lacks
clear definition.[10] Other countries have followed suit by
copying the United States. A majority of European countries,
form of physical disciplining is constituted as child abuse.[11]

In my experience, child abuse and spanking are two
completely separate issues. Spanking is strictly for the

---

[10] A helpful summary of the discussion is on the following web-page:
http://www.parents.com/toddlers-
preschoolers/discipline/spanking/spanking-discipline-debate/
[11] In the USA, it is currently legal to spank your child, or a child for
whom you are the legal guardian. Some states prohibit the spanking of
foster children.

purpose of helping the child to learn socially appropriate boundaries of behavior. Child abuse, on the other hand, is a willful act of inflicting arbitrary pain and injury on a child, provoked or unprovoked, without regard for the physical and emotional harm done to the child. Spanking is a form of physical discipline that has the best interest of the child in mind. For example, a judge who is sentencing an offender is not doing it because he is angry at the person, but because the person has violated the law. The parent, whom a judge is imitating, must not use this occasion to blow off steam because he or she is fed up or angry at the child. That is why it is very important that the child knows why he or she is being spanked. Remember, they were told beforehand in the various instruction phases, that this particular offense would be punished by spanking. There should be no surprises.

Is there an appropriate way of spanking? Having talked to many parents, we recommend that a moderately thin rod to be an appropriate tool for applying the discipline. The area of the body to be hit should be the covered buttocks only. In some schools, the spanking is applied to the palm of the hand. The teacher covers the wrist of the child with his own hand when applying the strokes to avoid accidentally hitting the wrist. Is there an appropriate time or reason for spanking? Spanking should be reserved for serious offenses such as lying, stealing, disrespecting the mother, willfully damaging someone else's property, vulgarity or sexual misbehavior. Spanking needs to be done with discretion and respect. This is not the time for humiliation. The number of strokes needs to be adjusted to the age and to the severity of the broken rule. Parents should avoid spanking the child in the child's own bedroom. The spanking could be in the parents' bedroom or in a neutral place. It should be done in private -

not in the presence of others. The most effective period for physical discipline is between the ages of three to eight. Ideally, the child has learned, by the latter age, to respond obediently to verbal instructions.

Our God has much to say about discipline, whether it be regarding a child, an adult or a nation. The Bible cautions fathers against committing two errors. The first error is mentioned in Ephesians 6:4 "Fathers, do not exasperate your children; instead, bring them up in the training and instruction of the Lord." Exasperation means to tire them out or wear them down with conflicting instructions and inconsistent times of discipline. This can happen when the parent doesn't understand the child's capability and may be ignorant of the developmental stage the child is in.

Often parents expect children to do better than they are really capable of. Sometimes children have not been given enough space to develop or even to practice their newly learned skills or motor activities. For example, a child two years of age is often referred to as being in the *terrible twos* stage of development. This sets the tone for expecting negative behavior from the child, when in fact it is a very exciting stage in which that two-year-old has finally mastered very complex social skills. Erik Erikson refers to the stage as developing *Autonomy vs. Shame*. The child can run, jump, hold a crayon, scribble, open drawers and empty them, say "no", run in the opposite direction from his mother, help her carry light things, and much more. Though a bit clumsy, he or she is very proud of being able to help. It's quite understandable that many accidents will happen as that little one is learning. How the parents respond to those accidents is crucial. If it is with anger, shouting and scolding, the child will learn to be ashamed and fearful when needing to step out into uncharted territory. If the parent responds with encouragement and understanding, the child will learn confidence in trying again until he can be autonomous.

Fathers should not micro-manage their teens, either. A son or daughter might be given too many details as to what to do, instead of being allowed to figure it out himself. This is a sign of not trusting them. It frustrates young people to no end!

The second error is mentioned in Colossians 3:21, "Fathers, do not embitter your children, or they will become discouraged." We embitter our children by treating them unjustly, by not listening to their point of view, by showing favoritism, by belittling them, and by not keeping our promises. Once teens have reached the point of complete discouragement, it is difficult to bring them back to a new level of enthusiasm. Remember – each child, of any age-group, carries the image of God within them from the day of conception. Any child deserves the same respect as any adult.

Usually, fathers tend to fall into these two traps because they have not communicated effectively with their wives. The mother has a greater sensitivity to a child's needs and capabilities. She senses a need beyond the physical observation. I remember times when my wife would encourage me to spend more individual time with our oldest son. Sometimes, she would caution me not to be so harsh or abrupt with the boys. She recognized my tendency to react to the external situation, while remaining unaware of the inner longing. I have learned to respond with more patience and kindness.

Today, there seems to be a re-discovery of the need for physical discipline. There is a recognition that it is essential in a young child's life for planting a healthy respect for self and authority. Evidence shows that children will become more secure as adults.[12] This is no surprise to a Bible believing parent. Here are only a few of the many verses in the Bible that instruct parents about discipline:

> "Whoever spares the rod hates their children, but the one who loves their children is careful to discipline them." (Proverbs 13:24)

> "Folly is bound up in the heart of a child, but the rod of discipline drives it far from him." (Proverbs 22:15)

> "Endure hardship as discipline; God is treating you as sons. For what son is not disciplined by his father? If you are not disciplined (and everyone undergoes discipline), then you are illegitimate children and not true sons. Moreover, we have all had human fathers who disciplined us and we respected them for it. How much more should we submit to the Father of our spirits and live? Our fathers disciplined us for a little while as they thought best; but God disciplines us for our good, that we may share in his holiness. No discipline seems pleasant at the time, but painful. Later on, however, it produces a harvest of

---

[12] Marjorie Gunnoe, professor of psychology at Calvin College in Grand Rapids, Michigan, said her study showed there was insufficient evidence to deny parents the freedom to determine how their children should be punished. She said: "The claims made for not spanking children fail to hold up. They are not consistent with the data. Those who had been smacked up to the age of six performed better in almost all the positive categories and no worse in the negatives than those never punished physically. Teenagers who had been hit by their parents from age seven to eleven were also found to be more successful at school than those not smacked but fared less well on some negative measures, such as getting involved in more fights.
(http://www.telegraph.co.uk/health/healthnews/6926823/Smacked-children-more-successful-later-in-life-study-finds.html)

righteousness and peace for those who have been trained by it." (Hebrews 12:7-11)

"Do not withhold discipline from a child; if you punish him with the rod, he will not die. Punish him with the rod and save his soul from death."
(Proverbs 23:13, 14)

"The rod of correction imparts wisdom, but a child left to himself disgraces his mother." (Proverbs 29:15)

Those who oppose spanking as a necessary means of discipline argue that the child learns to obey out of fear and not out of an inner motivation of right and wrong. In his book, *The Christian Family*, Larry Christenson addresses this argument:

"A spanking combines the twin aspects of love and fear, and in this it is patterned after our relationship to the Heavenly Father. Some people have trouble with the idea of fearing God because a certain brand of sentimental humanism has crept into our thinking. We think that love and fear cannot exist together. The Bible, however, consistently views love and fear as inseparable twins. The New Testament ... is replete with admonitions not only to love God, but also to fear Him"[13]

"Men of Israel, and you that fear God ..."
(Acts 13:16 NKJV).

"Cornelius, a devout man who feared God ..."
(Acts 10:1, 2 NKJV)

---

[13] Larry Christenson. *The Christian Family* . Bethany Press International, 1970

There is simply no replacement for effective, godly parental authority. Couples who seek the best for their children's future will stand together on the major issues. They will be faithful to instruct, practice and discipline their children. They will show the same love and respect towards their children as they have for each other. They will watch their children become responsible, confident adults.

SUMMARY

Every parent knows that children left to themselves can become troublemakers. The Bible tells us they need to be trained and to choose right over wrong. Training involves instruction, practice and discipline. The instruction phase includes teaching in age-appropriate language, with consequences for disobedience. The practice phase is creating opportunities for the child to rehearse the right thing. And the discipline phase is enforcing the good behavior by applying consequences to the wrong behavior.

Chapter Nine | Positions in the Family

"But I want you to realize that the head of every man is Christ, and the head of the woman is the man, and the head of Christ is God."
1 Corinthians 11:3

When someone applies for a new job, he or she usually takes some time to prepare. There may have been years of training behind that person and the new job. Before the person begins, he has carefully studied the qualifications needed. Then, a job description is set before him detailing most of the required work

****

When a couple plans to get married and comes to us for pre-marital counseling, we usually begin with the following explanation. The positions of wife and husband have existed long before you ever contemplated marriage. In fact, these positions were in the mind of God before creation; they were an integral part of God's blueprint for the social order. Some aspects of these positions are exactly the same, no matter which country or culture you live in. Yet, in the beauty of

God's plan they unfold in their unique expressions through you, as you both step into them. The responsibilities assigned to these positions of husband and wife are basically the same throughout the millennia. To discover them we need to consult the designer's manual - the Bible.

When God had created Eve, she became the first woman, the first wife and the first mother in all of creation. She was not at a loss as to the purpose for her existence. God had said before he created her that she was to be the helper to her husband. As the helper, she was not the one to lead them or to make the final decisions independently. She was to be submitted to the authority of her husband. (We will talk about the position of the husband later in the chapter.)

The *manual* says, in 1 Corinthians 11:3, that "the head of every wife is the husband." To some people that sounds oppressing. To others, especially to those who grew up in a well-functioning, happy family, it sounds like freedom. How one sees verse three in 1 Corinthians 11 depends on one's own experience. If, for example, the father of a young, married woman abused his authority in her original home, tyrannizing the mother and children, such a woman will remember that tension and fear. She may have told herself, *I'll never let myself be dominated by a man!* However, personal experiences do not determine the reality of the Bible. Why not? The Creator knew what he was doing. He knew how a marriage relationship would function best. Thank God that a young woman, who grew up in an abusive environment like that, will always be able to receive healing from her past and grow to enjoy her marriage.

In what areas is the wife a *helper* to her husband? There is the very obvious one of bearing him children. Only the woman is biologically able to grow a new life until birth. Only a mother has the very best nutrition for this new baby through breast feeding. As research has proven, the early bonding of the new-born with the mother is essential in establishing an emotional and physical security for the child. This early sense of safety and belonging is critical for building trusting relationships later.[14]

Looking at the place of the wife and mother as the helper to her husband and family generally, we are reminded of the words of Jesus when he said, "And I will pray to the Father, and He will give you another Helper, that He may abide with you." (John 14:16 NKJV) A closer look at the ministry of the Holy Spirit as our Helper reveals many similarities to the function of the wife. The different names of the Holy Spirit in the Bible describe his activities. He is referred to as the Spirit of truth. (John 14:17) In John 16:13 we read, "When the Spirit of truth has come, He will guide you into all truth." Other names given to the Holy Spirit in the Bible are Comforter, Counselor, Spirit of peace, Spirit of joy. It says that he convicts of sin, of righteousness, and of judgment (John 16:8), and he teaches us. (John 14:26)

It is evident that a mother fulfills these kinds of duties in the family. For example, who is the *comforter* in the home? Who kisses away the bumps and bruises of the toddler? Who rushes to the bedside of the four-year old after he had a bad dream with, "Shhh! It's okay. Mommy's here. Don't worry. You're going to be fine – just fine." And with a little humming, the child goes back to sleep, comforted! Who is

---

[14] Psychologist Mary Ainsworth, has elaborated on the work of John Bowlby's Attachment Theory and developed an experimental approach to demonstrate that early attachment of mother / child is pivotal in developing healthy, secure relationships even into adulthood. Ainsworth collaborated with Bowlby in the joint publication of their work, *Child Care and the Birth of Love* (1965).

always willing to explain and help with homework during elementary school? Mom, the teacher.

What about *counselor*? To whom do young teens go when advice is needed, their friends having turned against them or ostracized them? They talk to mom. They know that she can help because she *understands their feelings*.

What about *guidance*? Decisions have to be made for the years after high school. Even during those college years: to go here or there; to get involved in this class or that club, to take this sport or that one. Where does the late teen go? To mom.

And it's not only the children who go to mom for encouragement and comfort. The husband comes home from work exhausted, frustrated or disappointed. Who can understand him best? His wife!

It has been my experience that the wife is often a reliable influencer in also knowing God's will. If she is the one who is hesitant about the direction the family is taking, a red flag goes up and everybody stops to take a second look at the situation.

Another way a wife is the *helper* of her husband is by influencing him towards God. She can help him become a man of prayer and a man of the Word. Too often wives feel they need to step in and fulfill the office of the spiritual leader of the home because the husband had allowed himself to be distracted by seemingly more important activities: too much work, an all-consuming hobby, friends, sports or community involvements. However, God's real blessing rests on her helpership role, rather than her leadership role.

There is an incident in Exodus 4, about God's seriousness regarding a husband's spiritual leadership. In verses 24 to 26 we read, "At a lodging place on the way, the Lord met Moses and was about to kill him. But Zipporah took a flint knife, cut off her son's foreskin and touched Moses' feet with it. 'Surely you are a bridegroom of blood to me', she said. So the Lord let him alone." (At that time she said, *bridegroom of blood*, referring to circumcision.)

What does this peculiar little happening communicate? My version goes something like the following. Moses had finally accepted God's call to lead Israel out of Egypt. As he sets out on his journey, he takes his wife and son with him. They reach a place to spend the night, tired after a long day's journey. Suddenly, Moses experiences severe abdominal pain, a very high fever, and he can hardly breathe. It seems he's about to die. Zipporah, alarmed, cries out to God for her husband. It's then she remembers the argument they had had before they had left home about circumcising their son. As a matter of fact, ever since the boy had been born, they had argued about the need for him to be circumcised according to God's commandment. For some reason, Moses had dragged his feet, though his wife had reminded him over and over. In desperation now, she grabs the flint knife, and circumcises their son, fulfilling the spiritual duty of her husband. In this exception, the act actually restored God's favor.

Earlier, we said that the wife has authority from God to fulfill her role as the helper to her husband. I need to again point out that should the husband refuse her helpership, as Moses had done in the above account, he would be in rebellion to God. Why? Because God is the one who gave her the position of being the helper.

Now, let's see where husbands have authority to which their wives need to submit themselves. We understand that all authority comes from God. Where God entrusts us with responsibilities, he also anoints us with his authority to execute those responsibilities. What does God say to the husband regarding his role? In Ephesians 5:25-31, we read:

> "Husbands, love your wives, just as Christ loved the church and gave himself up for her to make her holy, cleansing her by the washing with water through the word, and to present her to himself as a radiant church, without stain or wrinkle or any other blemish, but holy and blameless. In this same way, husbands ought to love their wives as their own bodies. He who loves his wife loves himself. After all, no one ever hated his own body, but he feeds and cares for it, just as Christ does the church -- for we are members of his body. For this reason a man will leave his father and mother and be united to his wife, and the two will become one flesh."

The command God gives to the husbands is unmistakable. *"Love your wives as Christ loved the church and gave himself up for her."* It is here that the husband receives God's authority. It is to this kind of authority that the wife is to submit herself. In loving his wife, the, husband cancels the curse that was invoked on marriages in Genesis 3:16, "her desire will be for her husband, and he will rule over her."

Both, husband and wife have certain areas of responsibility to which God has given authority. Therefore, mutual submission is required. This idea is summed up in Ephesians 5:21. "Submit to one another out of reverence for Christ." Submission pre-supposes authority. God expects mutual submission to each other's areas of responsibility.

Husbands, who don't attempt to love their wives in a Christ-like fashion, have no basis for insisting on submission. They are living in disobedience. They forfeit the blessing God spoke over Adam and Eve in Genesis 1:28, "God blessed them and said to them, 'Be fruitful and increase in number; fill the earth and subdue it. Rule over the fish in the sea and the birds in the sky and over every living creature that moves on the ground.'" The evidence of men having lost that blessing is visible all around us. In home after home, parental authority has faded because husbands don't practice God's family order correctly.

In recent years we have seen that when God's ways were being ignored, God himself will raise up movements to bring things back to his original design. A notable example in the U.S. is one called *Promise Keepers*. This ministry, founded in 1990 by Bill McCartney, the head football coach at the University of Colorado, is a Christian organization for men. It is, "Dedicated to introducing men to Jesus Christ as their Savior and Lord, helping them to grow as Christians." Their publicized events tend to be mass rallies held at football stadiums or similar venues. Promise Keepers' most notable event was its *Stand in the Gap: A Sacred Assembly of Men* open-air gathering at the National Mall in Washington, D.C. on October 4, 1997. It was reported to be the largest gathering of men in the history of the USA. Promise Keepers has continued to grow worldwide, welcoming men from all churches as well as unchurched men.[15]

Another notable ministry called Father School started in 1995 in Seoul, South Korea, at Duranno Bible College. The mission was to end what the Father School guidebook calls, "The growing national epidemic of abusive, ineffective and absentee fathers." In 2000, Father School spread from Korea to the United States, and the program — partly a 12-step recovery program, partly a Christian ministry — was then

---

[15] http://en.wikipedia.org/wiki/Promise_Keepers

tailored to meet the needs of Korean immigrant fathers dealing with Americanized kids who wondered why their fathers weren't more like the touchy-feely dads they saw on TV. Since then, Father School has exploded. It operates out of 57 American cities and has graduated nearly 200,000 men worldwide.[16]

Marriage and family, in its original design, will never become obsolete. "So will my word be which goes forth from my mouth; It will not return to me empty, without accomplishing what I desire, and without succeeding in the matter for which I sent it." (Isaiah 55:11)

SUMMARY

When God designed marriage and family, He gave each a functional place that provided identity and meaning to them. The husband was assigned the place of headship, the wife was assigned the role of helpership, and the children were to grow in obedience and maturity into adulthood within that bond of love. This would guarantee harmony and peace. Throughout history, the family has been challenged by the enemy, but God is ultimately in control. He will not allow his plans to be overthrown.

---

[16] http://www.nytimes.com/2011/05/08/magazine/mag-08Here-t.html?_r=0

Chapter Ten | God's Social Microcosm

"If anyone does not know how to manage his own family, how can he take care of God's church?" 1 Timothy 3:5

On one of our trips we were invited by the staff of a government agency in a non-Christian country to hold a seminar dealing with Family Relationships. At the beginning of the week I asked a simple question, "What is a family?"

Most people answer: a married man and woman with their children. But this time one person answered, "The family is the social microcosm of society." Pleasantly surprised, I asked her, "Could you please explain that?" "Well," she said, "The family is the smallest social unit or cell of society. Whatever happens in that cell determines the health of the nation."

She was right. In an earlier chapter, we saw that from the beginning God intended the family to be the channel by which he would communicate his character and his ways, from one generation to the next generation. The Bible gives an example in Genesis 18:19. God was looking for a person to whom he could entrust confidential information about Sodom and Gomorrah and chose Abraham, "I have known him, in order that he may command his children and his household after him, that they keep the way of the Lord, to do righteousness and justice, that the Lord may bring to Abraham what He has spoken to him." (NKJV)

A nation functions, in many ways, like the family except on a larger level. The family, as a social unit of society, becomes a political entity. Remember God told Adam and Eve in Genesis 1:28 to "subdue the earth and have dominium over it." To *subdue and have dominion* included every area of human engagement in God's creation. Whatever constructive activities that human beings would be capable of and gifted in, they were to use. It is true that through the Fall, when man discovered that in his selfishness he could also exploit creation, decay came into creation. However, through Christ's finished work on the cross, Satan and sin were conquered. Thus, God opened the door to reclaiming what the devil had stolen or destroyed. Jesus himself explained how this should work:

"All authority in heaven and on earth has been given to me. Therefore go and make disciples of all nations, baptizing them in the name of the Father and of the Son and of the Holy Spirit, and teaching them to obey everything I have commanded you. And surely I will be with you always, to the very end of the age." (Matthew 28:18-20)

That moment, recorded in Matthew, is known as the Great Commission. It has been the mandate for Christians throughout the ages to take the Good News of God's love to the entire world. As people would accept the Good News (that their sins were to be forgiven by surrendering their lives to Jesus Christ), they would be baptized and taught ALL that God had commanded from the beginning. God looked to the family as His training ground for raising up men and women to perpetuate truth into every domain of society. Today, maybe as never before, God is still looking for families to accomplish this. God needs families who are intentional in training up their children. If families languish, so does the society. To understand this better, let's look at the functional structure of a nation.

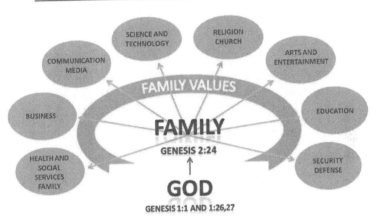

FAMILY, THE SOCIAL MICROCOSM OF A NATION

In the above illustration, the family is the smallest social cell in the microcosm of a nation.

From the beginning, nations have been very much part of God's plan. As it says in Acts 17:26-27, "From one man he made every nation of men that they should inhabit the whole earth, and he determined the times set for them and the exact places where they should live. He did this so that men would seek Him."

Every nation is made of small building blocks, just as every living organism is made of millions of small microscopic cells that together enable the life of that organism. When these cells are healthy the organism is doing well. When cells are deteriorating through disease like cancer, the whole organism is in trouble. Humanity's history is largely dominated by the interactions of nations. We've come to speak of nation-building, *nation-states*, national identity, self-determination and so forth. But, what exactly is a *nation*? Basically, a nation is a group of people who live in a defined geographic area. What makes this group of people a nation is that they have a set of shared values and beliefs. These values and beliefs become customs. Customs become laws. To function collectively, people choose individuals whose task it is to implement their laws. These individuals become the *government* of a nation.

They form institutions of governing: law-making bodies, executive offices, judicial systems and others. These institutions give rise to *departments* or *ministries*. Departments are empowered and entrusted with specific areas of responsibility over various aspects of the life of the nation. These may include health, social welfare, family affairs, education, finance, transportation, religion, communication, culture, the arts, commerce, science and technology, international affairs, defense and national security, to name a few.

The various departments of our collective governments mirror what we learn about the world in our childhood. For example, we learn about the importance of Social Welfare as we interact with our family, share our possessions, protect and not harm each other and comfort one another. The first institution a child observes in the family is the legislative institution. Children have first-hand opportunities to see good or bad government in action by watching parents make decisions. How do they organize the home, decide their money matters, plan future events, handle creativity? In 1 Timothy 3:1-7, the Apostle Paul gives a list of qualifications that a man in a leadership position should meet. Among these requirements Paul asks, "If anyone does not know how to manage his own family well and see that his children obey him with proper respect, how can he take care of God's church?" In other words, every man is given the responsibility to govern himself and his family well first of all.

As children grow older, parents will involve them in the decision-making process. For example, the family of believers will train children in knowing God, how to hear and obey God, how to study the Bible, how to find principles to live by, how to intercede for those inside and outside the family. These all require making good choices. Boys and girls need to take their turns in the family devotional times. Most of the time parents think too little of the spiritual hunger of young children and only try to draw them into worshipping God with them when they are teens. However, because of all the other demands on them, this is usually a poor time to start training in spirituality. All this training is the part of the legislature of the family.

Parents can train their children in the area of management by putting them in charge of certain projects without looking over their shoulders. For example, they can be asked to make plans for a sibling's birthday party or to put on a talent show or planning for a holiday or making hospital visits. Through proper management (government) training, children will be practicing legislative responsibilities.

When children learn from their parents where money comes from and how it is spent, they are learning about stewardship, tithing, generosity, care in buying and honesty in selling. They receive spending money appropriate for their ages and learn about finances: how to be accountable to others, how to spend money, how to keep track of where the money is spent, and how to save it. Even at an early age, children can be taught to set up a budget and live within the boundaries of their *income*. Learning these money matters early on will help them to avoid financial disasters later. We could call it early training in Finance and Business.

Another *department* children learn about is Communication and the Arts. Children learn how to communicate with integrity, kindness and honesty by making phone calls, by giving short speeches, texting simple memos, writing thank-you notes, responding effectively to Facebook or e-mails and by writing business letters. These days, it has become easy to communicate with photos, videos and Skyping via cell phones.

In the Arts, there are numerous opportunities to teach the appreciation of nature and beauty. Children should receive some lessons to develop skill in drawing, music, sculpturing, drama, photography, dancing or painting. Giftings in children are usually discovered at an early age. They can easily be encouraged and supported by further training. Practicing the fine arts are such valuable opportunities to build confidence and self-expression. If early childhood years are not used to train children in their giftings, the children will be ill-prepared for their adolescent years, when self-consciousness and inferiority are major blocks.

Preparing for the Department of Education during childhood is an obvious good illustration. Educating children rests primarily with the parents according to Scripture. In Deuteronomy 6:6-9, Moses exhorts the nation to not neglect instructing their children and children's children in the ways of God. He says:

"These commandments that I give you today are to be upon your hearts. Impress them on your children. Talk about them when you sit at home and when you walk along the road, when you lie down and when get up. Tie them as symbols on your hands and bind them on your foreheads. Write them on the doorframes of your houses and on your gates."

In other words, Moses is saying, *don't miss any opportunity to teach your children who God is and what he says.* In Proverbs 6:20 Solomon says, "My son, keep your father's commands and do not forsake you mother's teaching." Unfortunately, too many Christian parents are not involved in their children's education. They prefer to put them into a public nursery, preschool, kindergarten, public elementary school, middle school, high school, and public college. What have the children learned? How much about the ways and character of God are in the curricula of these public institutions? Should we be honest? Next to nothing. How strong is their faith at the end of these years? If there is any faith in God left when our young people graduate from public education, it is unusual. Too many who have walked through the *temples* of our educational system come out worshipping education, status, money, themselves, talents, success, their own abilities, or other people. This has replaced the study and understanding of our precious Creator God, the Number ONE in the universe.

Studying the departments of a nation, in the context of *family* underscores the importance of the family as the *building block*. Christian parents have the privilege of training their sons and daughters in understanding the responsibilities of a nation from a Biblical perspective. Not only will they become responsible adults, but they will be healthy contributors to and leaders of our nations. After all, "the fear of the Lord is the beginning of wisdom; all who follow his precepts have good understanding. To him belongs eternal praise." (Psalm 111:10)

SUMMARY

Every nation is made of small building blocks – small social cells called families. Healthy nations must have healthy families to survive. This is God's original plan and it has not changed.

Chapter Eleven | Hope for Families in Disarray

"After I looked things over, I stood up and said to the nobles, the officials and the rest of the people, 'Don't be afraid of them. Remember the Lord, who is great and awesome, and fight for your families, your sons and your daughters, your wives and your homes.'" Nehemiah 4:14

In the previous chapter, we discussed God's plan for the nation via the family. There seems to be an ever widening gap between the ideal family and the families functioning today. However, in this chapter we would like to share hope for the malfunctioning family. In chapter seven, we saw the detrimental influences that strongholds of the mind can have on a husband and wife relating to one another. The strongholds of false beliefs we discussed in that chapter were fabrications that had set themselves up against the true knowledge of what God would say about us. (2 Cor. 10:3-5)
One of the most influential components of our personality (or soul) is our emotions. Emotions do not perform in a vacuum; they do not stand alone in our personality make-up. They always act in sync with our thoughts. Thoughts are subject to our will, the third component of our personality. I can make a mental decision - telling my will to do something. Therefore, if emotions are evoked by thoughts, my thoughts

can exercise my will's authority over these emotions. Thoughts give the emotions permission to stay or go. What we believe about ourselves, as well as the universe, directly impacts our feelings.

Emotions are not the thoughts, but the thoughts bring up the emotions. For example, when an important person in your life tells you that you are a failure or that you will never amount to anything, immediately, a bundle of emotions are aroused in you. You may feel very sad, discouraged, fearful, rejected, or angry. In other words, your *will* gives you the permission to accept the emotions that were evoked by those remarks. These emotions are entirely your own. Nobody else can own them. You have complete authority over them. The words that were dumped on you came from another source, outside of you, but the emotions came from within you. So, what will you do with them?

Some situations can lead to a major existential crisis. This was exactly the case of one of our friends. His own father had made the above remarks to him and dismissed him from the family business in front of all the other employees. The young man stood at the brink of committing suicide. However, through a Christian friend, he gave his life to Jesus instead. The teaching and personal ministry he and his family received from the body of Christ provided deep healing. In time, he could rebuild the foundation of his life and no longer depend on the approval of others to know who he was, or what he could be. He learned to appreciate the way God saw him. He learned that God had "a specific future and a hope" for him.[17] Today, he is a wonderful businessman greatly appreciated by his employees. He is also a loving husband and father.

---

[17] Jeremiah 29:11

Let's go back to Glenn and his wife, Erica. Let's imagine them driving on the highway. Erica is quiet with her thoughts. She's almost in tears, feeling that Glenn just doesn't appreciate her. He had been yelling at her. Often she would have serious questions about his love for her. Glenn on the other hand wonders why Erica never has any confidence in him, nor in any of his abilities, including driving! Both ride in silence, feeling unappreciated, full of anger, rejection, and self-pity. Suddenly, the car in front of them swerves out of control to avoid a huge boulder and crashes, instead, into an oncoming car. Immediately, Glenn pulls to the side and dials for help. Erica is out of the car in a flash, running over to the accident scene, to figure out how she could assist. They spend over an hour helping the injured, covering them with blankets, setting up emergency flares and directing cars, until the ambulance and police arrive. All along they keep talking to the injured people in calm reassuring voices. Finally, after the ambulances leave, they get back into their car and slowly drive on.

What happened to their emotions of self-pity, rejection and abandonment? Do you think that after this dramatic distraction they would go back to their earlier emotions? Definitely not. Such an incident clearly illustrates that our emotions are fleeting; we can dismiss them at will or we can give them permission to stay.

Some people get so *buddy-buddy* with negative emotions that those emotions have become their best friends. These negative emotions may cripple them and make them ineffective in their day-to-day activities, but since they have become their identity, the people continue to give them a lot of mileage, with extra special attention to self-pity. Giving up these crippling emotions would be extremely dangerous because they are afraid of the new, unfamiliar life-style on the other side. So, they are stuck in an unhealthy and often toxic rut.

Negative emotions hinder relationships. They are very destructive. Therefore, it is our goal in counseling to help a person move into a better level of functioning. The apostle Paul writes in 1 Thessalonians 5:18, "Be joyful always." In other words, give little or no room to negative emotions in habitual indulgence. The Bible clearly states that it is within our power to direct our emotions from negativity to a higher level. In Colossians 3:8, we read, "But now you must also rid yourselves of all such things as these: anger, rage, malice, slander, and filthy language from your lips." And also in verse twelve " Therefore, as God's chosen people, holy and dearly loved, clothe yourselves with compassion, kindness, humility, gentleness and patience." Some people may ask, "But what if the circumstances are so horrible that there is no reason for having any positive feelings?"

Emotions are never a reliable indicator of where things are at from a larger perspective. At best, they give us a subjective conclusion of the situation in which we are living. That is why we need to step out of that moment in time and view it in the context of the larger picture, remembering God's eternal presence. He promises to never leave us or forsake us! His infinite power is available to help each person overcome any hindrance. Our emotions ought to follow that perspective, rather than enabling our past negative thinking.

In conclusion, emotions are not logical; they don't think; they merely respond to thoughts. Thoughts merely respond to circumstances. Negative emotions can be put aside at a moment's notice when a new circumstance enters the picture. Can they not also be put aside through an act of the will? Of course they can! With our God-given ability to choose, it is indeed possible.

Much of today's counseling is focused on emotions, particularly on dealing with resentment, anger and depression. Articles and books have been written on managing our emotions. Researchers have directed their attention to the science of genetics to look for components that might be the cause of anger. They have called on the multi-billion dollar pharmaceutical industry to come to the rescue. In Ephesians 4:26, we are warned not to let anger lead us into sin. The assumption is that anger is a human response to certain situations, but it is the angry person's responsibility to control the anger and dismiss it before the "sun goes down." Otherwise, we give the devil a foothold and allow him to make the emotion the leader instead of the follower.

Giving full vent to anger is the mark of fools, whereas keeping one's self under control is the mark of a wise man. (Proverbs 29:11) Expressing uncontrolled anger in families is the source of enormous grief and very often it goes together with alcoholism. The Bible tells the would-be alcoholic to control his alcohol intake. For example, it says, "Do not get drunk on wine, which leads to debauchery." (Ephesians 5:18) Recently, some friends of ours quit their alcoholism because of a certain medical prognosis. Without any special medication or outside help they just stopped. They had been fairly heavy drinkers for many of their adult years. So, although our friends are not Christians, they no longer drink. Imagine how much more we, who know the Lord, can do when we rely on God's help!

So far, we have not given attention to the *root* of all negative emotions: fear. Why is fear the root of all negative emotions? Simply, because it is the opposite of love. In 1

John 4:8 we are reminded that God is love and in verse 18 we are told "perfect love casts out all fear." At what point was fear allowed to have such a universal presence? In chapter three of Genesis, after Adam and Eve had decided to obey Satan, God responded by casting the couple out of the Garden of Eden, lest they would also eat of the tree of life in their sinful condition and live eternally. (Genesis 3:22, 23) Therefore, as sin separates us from God, who is the Giver or Root of all *true* love, (Isaiah 59:2; 64:7) it also separated us from loving one another.

It is my conviction that in love's place, the opposite emotion – fear moved into the Garden of Eden. We might say it is the *motherboard,* or the *operating system,* of the kingdom of Satan. Philosophers call it *Weltangst*[18], an existential anxiety that is always prevalent in us – our insecurity about anything or anyone. It is a general uncertainty about the future. Some of the root-fears we struggle with, especially if we do not know God, are: the fear of dying; the fear of aloneness or abandonment; the fear of hurt or harm; the fear of inadequacy; the fear of failure; the fear of the unknown; and the fear of insignificance. People use a tremendous amount of energy, even creativity, in their struggles to hide or overcome these fears. Think of the *workaholic* who strives to overcome his fear of failure; or the student who is the *meticulous perfectionist* battling the fear of inferiority; or the wife who controls her husband through her manipulative *sicknesses* to overcome her fear of abandonment.

These behaviors, and many others, have the potential of escalating into all forms of mental problems – from mild depression to psychotic breakdowns. The workaholic, for

---

[18] Oswald Spengler, *The Decline of the West,* 2 Vols., trans. Charles Francis Atkinson, (New York: Alfred A. Knopf, 1922)

example, may develop delusions of losing all he has worked so hard for. So, he hoards all his possessions and builds secret compartments to hide his money. Or an artist might become paranoid about others trying to steal his creative ideas and accomplishments, and therefore refuses to allow any people to see or even buy his work. There is the escalating fear in the perfectionist college student who sets his goals so high that he can never reach them. Or think of the high school student who deals with the fear of failure by rejecting herself through anorexia, a hate/love relationship with herself. On the one hand she punishes herself and wants to do away with herself, plagued by suicide wishes. On the other hand, she loves herself so much; she has an overwhelming desire to be slim and attractive.

Fear is the strategy of our enemy to wear us down. It is a force that demands action against it or we become paralyzed by it. In the Bible, the word *fear* is translated from the Greek *phobio*. Psychologists have identified hundreds of different phobias. Not all behaviors used in covering up fears are bad. For example, a single man who ventures to Uganda and establishes a group home for AIDS children might have been motivated to do so by his fear of sickness. Or the single woman who chooses to adopt children may have been operating sacrificially, while covering up her not-so-conscious fear of being alone in her old age. Both are self-motivated in their actions by their underlying fears, yet they have funneled their fears into helping others.

The ultimate solution to fear, however, is perfect love. This healing love can only come from God, since he is the only one who is perfect. Therefore, knowing God is a prerequisite to becoming healed from fears. No therapy, counseling, or medication can heal the fear in a person's heart except the love of God. In his letter to the Roman Christians, Paul writes that "God has poured out his love into our hearts by the Holy Spirit." (Romans 5:5) Just like the strongholds in our minds that have to be demolished, residual fears in our hearts must be radically dealt with, in order to enter into freedom and peace.

After mental or emotional strongholds have lost their strangle-hold on our lives, our focus will turn from self to others. Only then can we be free to enjoy this verse in Matthew, "Let your light shine before men, that they may see your good deeds and praise your Father in heaven." (Matthew 5:16)

SUMMARY

We have mentioned how families can receive healing for their damaged emotions. When we give permission to our emotions to lead our ways, we very quickly discover that we are on a roller-coaster that keeps us going in circles. One day we feel up, the next we feel down. Fears become the barrier that stops us from doing things. As we allow the love of our heavenly Father to enter into our lives, fear loses its control on us and we regain a healthy confidence.

Chapter Twelve | The Heart of the Family

"Above all else, guard your heart, for everything you do flows from it."
Proverbs 4:23

Any problem in relationships, whether in families or otherwise, can be traced back to problems of the heart. In the New Testament letter to the Hebrews, the writer cautions his readers, "See to it, brothers, that none of you has a sinful, unbelieving heart that turns away from the living God." (Hebrews 3:12) Jesus says in no uncertain terms in Mark 7:21-23, "For from within, out of men's hearts come evil thoughts, sexual immorality, theft, murder, adultery, greed, malice, deceit, lewdness, envy, slander, arrogance and folly. All these evils come from inside and make a man 'unclean'."

The source of destructive behaviors, according to Jesus, is in *the heart*. Therefore, a change of the heart is required for lasting and constructive solutions to marriage problems.

To begin with, we need to ask the Holy Spirit to illuminate our hearts, so that we can identify any root- fear on which so many of our behavioral patterns have been built. The deception here is that we firmly believe that our adopted behaviors can adequately control the fears that harass us. It's like Adam and Eve wearing fig leaves to cover their physical nakedness in response to their newly-discovered fear of God.

The truth is, controlling and concealing ourselves to cope with fear is ineffectual in the long run. When the behaviors we have adopted fail to remove the fears, insecurity enters our spirit and registers as *guilt*. We feel we have done something wrong. But why do we feel this guilt? The Bible tells us that "all have sinned," (Romans 3:23) which means *all* have broken God's perfect law, and therefore *all* of us feel guilty. In Romans 1:20 we read, "For since the creation of the world God's invisible qualities—his eternal power and divine nature—have been clearly seen, being understood from what has been made, so that people are without excuse."

Whether our knowledge of God comes from observing His creation or whether our conscience is responding to the Law of God written on our hearts (Romans 2:14-15), we need God's erasing of our sinfulness. A proper response to guilt is turning to Jesus Christ, who has paid the price for our sin and guilt. He offers us his clothing of righteousness in place of our sin-stained clothing.

As I pointed out in the previous chapter, fear is at the root of all negative emotions. It alternately breeds and is fed by other feelings of envy, resentment, anger, hatred, rage, distrust, paranoia, depression and others. When given the space, these emotions can reduce us to a low level of family and social functioning. They also interfere with a vital faith in God. In some instances, negative dispositions may have been passed on from previous generations. We are able to identify such patterns of *generational fear*, and can break their influence on us through the power of the blood of Jesus. They will then cease to exercise their authority over us.

Fears are rooted in unbelief. One upholds the other. We know this because the Word of God emphasizes that perfect love drives out fears. As we believe the Bible, we know that God's love has the power to deliver us from all fears. Because fears function as inhibitors, they block revelation from God and keep us from hearing his voice. When we don't believe Jesus, the Bible calls this unbelief *sin*. The challenge is to choose to deal with unbelief at the root level. This would mean repenting of that sin (turning completely away from it) after the Holy Spirit has brought it to our awareness. Of equal importance, is that we follow repentance with accepting the forgiveness that God grants us. God does really forgive each particular sin. He actually removes the guilt. We can become *totally* free!

Sometimes our foe operates in a similar style. It is called *false guilt*. False guilt is often Satan's continuous weapon to keep us in an on-going bondage. False guilt tells you that you have not been forgiven, that you are still guilty of that same sin and deserve to be punished. The fact is this: the punishment of our sin was already applied to Jesus on the cross, when Jesus "became sin" for us.[19] It is the complete and amazing truth. When Satan says that you must prove yourself to God by doing some good or difficult deed in order to overcome your guilt, it is a shameful lie! Do NOT give in to it. It is *false guilt* speaking. The Word of God is clear. The Apostle John writes in 1 John 1:9 "If we confess our sins, He is faithful and just to forgive us our sins and cleanse us from all unrighteousness." Righteousness (or right living) is restored to us the moment we repent! Following our

---

[19] "God made him who had no sin to be sin for us, so that in him we might become the righteousness of God." (2 Corinthians 5:21)

repenting, our real guilt is done away with and we are free to enjoy our freedom from the past.

In the Bible, fear is called a spirit. It came right out of Satan's hordes into God's creation when Adam and Eve agreed to believe Satan instead of God. Remember how Adam responded when God asked, "Where are you?" It was, "I was afraid because I was naked; and I hid." In Romans 8:15, the Lord tells us, "For you did not receive a spirit that makes you a slave again to fear, but you received the Spirit of sonship. By him we cry, *Abba, Father.*"

The absolutely beautiful thing we see here, is, that the revelation of God as our Father, brings about the solution to the fear problem both intellectually, in the abstract; and personally in the emotional realm. God, who IS love, comes right into our hearts to deliver us and heal us from the torment of the *Weltangst* and all of its tendrils. What an awesome privilege we Christians have. And those of us who are fathers can bring the love of THE Father (of all fathers) into our marriage and family. How happy God must be when we become whole and use our wholeness to help others!

SUMMARY

What comes out of the heart, the good, the bad or the ugly, will shape each individual life and ultimately the life of the family. Therefore, through repentance before God, we must cleanse our heart from former patterns of fear and allow God to fill us with his love. Then fear cannot find a place in our individual lives or families.

Chapter Thirteen | Communication

"Finally, brothers and sisters, whatever is true, whatever is noble, whatever is right, whatever is pure, whatever is lovely, whatever is admirable - if anything is excellent or praiseworthy - think about such things." Philippians 4:8

Surveys of divorced couples and those who experience marital problems on a continuous basis, place *poor or no communication* at the top of the list of reasons for their marriage break-down. One gets the impression that if they could learn to talk more and share on a deeper level, all would be well. The assumption is that communication consists merely of verbal messages passed on from one person to another. It has been our experience that when couples have communication problems, it is not about the verbal messages, but about the sources from which they originate. After all, communication is only a tube through which something is funneled.

In Mark 7:21, Jesus points out, "For from within, out of men's hearts come evil thoughts, sexual immorality, theft, murder..." In the previous chapter, we discussed how thoughts produce feelings: evil thoughts produce bad, negative feelings – and encouraging thoughts produce uplifting feelings. If we give in to the evil desires of our hearts, they will lead to evil thoughts which we will speak out. The result is that others around us will be hurt. Is it any wonder, that others react with equally evil thoughts or choose to withdraw from any further interaction? The real problem with these couples in marital crisis is not the poor communication, but the negative feelings and secrets they have been harboring.

When my wife and I counsel, we frequently take the couple back to the beginning of their relationship. We listen to them tell us how they first met, how their dating progressed and how they spent those months before the wedding. Invariably, their tolerance for each other's differences was very high. Once married, things gradually changed. What had seemed unique or funny became a source of irritation. He had wanted his coffee black (because of the calories in cream and sugar), she had preferred cream and sugar; he preferred to get up early and go for a swim before work, she liked to sleep in; he snored, she didn't and was easily awakened; she liked to meet friends at Starbucks, he called it an intrusion on their private life; he liked to have sex in the early morning, she preferred the late evenings. The list goes on and on. Slowly their feelings for each other cooled off to the point of ending up in an argument over every tiny issue.

One couple we were counseling, John and Kelly, sat in my office and looked at each other in amazement when we had reached this point in the discussion. They weren't sure whether they should laugh or cry. It sounded so silly, so ridiculous! Yet, that was exactly where they were at. They couldn't see how things could ever change.

"Well, where do you want to go from here?" I asked them at the end. "Do you want to continue the downward-path or work hard bringing about changes?"

"I'm so ashamed of myself," Kelly finally said in tears. "I really do love John. I just don't know what to do to get close to him anymore."

"How about you, John? What are your feelings for Kelly?" I challenged him.

"I really wouldn't want to be married to anybody else. I just wish I could change myself and not get so darnn irritated by all those silly things," John said, very sincerely.

"We appreciate what both of you just spoke out," I told them. "Did you notice that you expressed warm and caring feelings for one another? It seems to me you had gotten caught up in a fear-struggle. Maybe you thought you would look weak by giving in? Maybe you feared that the other person would take unfair advantage of you?" They both nodded, thoughtfully. "There may have been some connection to past experiences. In our next session, we'll talk more about those things. There is a verse in the Bible about love covering a multitude of sins.[20] It seems, the things that irritated you about the other person were not necessarily sins, so, why don't we simply say, *love covers a multitude of differences?*"

"Sounds good," Kelly responded.

"And 1 John 4:18 says, perfect love cast out or drives out fear because fear has to do with punishment. Would you be willing to first individually meditate on these two verses this week? Write down what the Holy Spirit shows you and be willing to share them in my office next week. Would you be willing to try something new in your relationship?"

---

[20] "Above all, love each other deeply, because love covers over a multitude of sins." (1 Peter 4:8)

"Anything," John replied. "Our way of dealing with conflict so far hasn't worked. So, I'm ready for something new." Kelly agreed.

"Okay. For the next week, every time you come up against an incident that used to arouse resentment or irritation, try to take control over it. Command it to get out of your heart. Remind yourself that your love, through Christ, for your spouse covers the stuff that made you angry and let it go. Express something affirming to your spouse, instead. Take him or her into your arms and thank God silently for your marriage. Would you do that?"

Both looked a bit sheepish, but they agreed to try.

When we saw John and Kelly a week later, they couldn't stop expressing their excitement over the new atmosphere at home. It had actually worked. They had had the best week in a long, long time. They eagerly shared what God had showed them through the verses without interruptions or put-downs.

This should not come as a surprise to us because the Bible is full of encouraging verses to help us in our daily living. For example, "Speak to one another with psalms, hymns and spiritual songs. Sing and make music in your heart to the Lord, always giving thanks to God the Father for everything, in the name of our Lord Jesus Christ." (Ephesians 5:19) Positive thoughts bring about positive emotions.

Many of today's psychologists argue that to get rid of negative thoughts, one needs to speak them out. They claim that healthy thinking comes by confronting the other person with what he/she really thinks of them. In fact, the opposite happens when following that theory: negative thoughts propagate negative emotions, and the negative emotions propagate negative and destructive behavior. Many relationships have been damaged, some beyond repair, using this *let it all hang-out* method.

One could ask whether a person would prefer to dig through a trash bin to see all that is in it before it goes to the dump? We wouldn't do that, so why would we want to re-live the trash of our past before we dump it at the foot of the cross? The apostle Paul says, "One thing I do: Forgetting what is behind and straining toward what is ahead, I press on toward the goal." (Philippians 3:13, 14)

SUMMARY

Genuine communication is a core value in healthy, intimate marriages. This level of intimacy is a heart matter, where love and respect for each other resides. A necessary change of heart sets us free of past trash and failures. It needs to be a change that recharges the heart with the love that heals, binds together, and covers the minute offenses.

Chapter Fourteen | The Compatibility Factor

"Every good and perfect gift is from above, coming down from the Father of the heavenly lights, who does not change like shifting shadows."
James 1:17

High on the list of reasons given by couples for trouble in their marriage is the so-called *incompatibility* factor. Young, engaged couples coming for pre-marital counseling often want to know whether they are compatible. They would like to take personality inventories that can predict whether their relationship will have a chance of making it and the assumption here, is that some personalities are so opposite that divorce is inevitable.

Following that line of thinking, one would have to conclude that two adults with different personalities could never be roommates or flat-mates. Siblings with differing personalities would inevitably create too many problems in families. Friends with different interests could never stay friends. Many young people, out of fear, buy into the unbiblical notion that they have to live together before they get married to see whether they are compatible. They ignore extensive research findings that consistently show that the divorce rate among couples who cohabit before marriage is significantly higher than for those couples that do not.[21] The same is true for couples who have lived a promiscuous life before marriage. They, too, show a significantly higher divorce rate. Promiscuity (fornication and other sexual sins) is never a part of God's preparation for marriage.

By *incompatibility*, people today generally mean differences in intelligence; differences in education; introversion vs. extroversion; differences in professions or occupations; social status differences; physical appearance; ethnicity; age differences; differences of religious backgrounds or outlooks on life; and different interests in sports, music, tastes, or hobbies.

Being compatible versus being incompatible is a matter of the mind and heart. If I latch on to a negative thought about a certain trait in my spouse, then that trait has the potential of becoming an element for incompatibility. However, if I act in the Lord's wisdom to renounce that negative thought and turn away from the negative feelings it generates, I have restored the compatibility between us. What some people may view as complementary in a relationship, others may view as dangerous or divisive!

The difference is one of perspective. It turns out that God is more concerned with inward characteristics than outward appearances, "People look at the outward appearance, but the Lord looks at the heart." (1 Samuel 16:7) A couple may wake up one morning and focus on one or two differences and begin to feel bad about their marriage.

---

[21]http://divorce.lovetoknow.com/Divorce_Statistics_and_Living_Togeth er

Is it the marriage or the negative thoughts and feelings about their differences? In my experience there is no universal standard by which to predict compatibility. After a good day, we look at our differences and say, "Cool! Aren't we blessed to be so different! It certainly enriches our marriage!" On a bad day, we may say exactly the opposite. God's promise still stands that "the two will become one." Celebrating our differences beats fighting them. Since marriage is God's invention, he will certainly guide us through the confusing, contradictory, emotional world we live in.

What should be of greater focus, is a couple's *spiritual compatibility*. After all, at the center of a healthy marriage is the worship of God. That's why the Bible insists, "Do not be yoked together with unbelievers. For what do righteousness and wickedness have in common? Or what fellowship can light have with darkness? What harmony is there between Christ and Belial[22]? Or what does a believer have in common with an unbeliever?" (2 Corinthians 6:14-15)

In marriages where the husband and wife are of different religions, the house is divided and they go in different directions, with different values. For example, the wife goes to church on Sunday morning, whereas the husband watches sports on TV; the husband goes to parties where there is a lot of drinking, the wife prefers to visit with like-minded believers; the husband likes to have regular devotional times with the children, reading the Bible together; the wife dismisses it as silliness and has her yoga meditation at that time. These differences cause much friction and could easily

---

[22]A demon mentioned frequently in apocalyptic literature: identified in the Christian tradition with the devil or Satan
(http://www.thefreedictionary.com/Belial)

lead to divorce. One man we know promised his fiancée she could continue her Christian beliefs. However, after marriage, he insisted she convert to Islam. God is definite about the warning, "Do not be yoked together with unbelievers." If a couple is already married and one of them becomes a Christian, their spiritual incompatibility can be overcome by much prayer and fasting (Mark 9:29), but it often includes pain and frustration.

Spiritual compatibility includes a husband and wife who relate to each other as believers in Christ. In Colossians 3:14 Paul writes, "Above all these (referring to a list of virtues) put on love which binds all things together." (NKJV) Instead of analyzing our marriage on the basis of our personal differences, the Lord directs our attention to our spiritual compatibility. Since God is love and our source of love (1 John 4:8, 16), we, who have been created in his image, can engage in this most strengthening and fulfilling activity, namely that of loving one another. How? A good start to achieving spiritual congruity is to daily study the Word of God together. In addition to reading God's Word together, the more a couple prays with each other, where each partner has a turn, the stronger and faster the spiritual growth will be.

SUMMARY

Diversity is the mark of God's creation. Diversity in marriage enriches life. To the extent we appreciate each other's differences; we will learn to love each other more deeply. This is clearly the best answer to questions of *compatibility*. It is essential that couples worship the one true God, through Jesus Christ, our Savior, who is the Creator of all.

Chapter Fifteen | The Function of Beams

"Blessed are the merciful for they shall obtain mercy." Matthew 5:7

Buildings that have stood the test of time are set on a firm foundation with walls that are resilient to adverse weather conditions and earthquakes. Comparing a marriage to a building under construction, we too have to choose quality materials that protect and secure against all kinds of adversities. Let's look at some of these proven materials. We begin with a beam called *mercy*.

In practical terms the word *mercy* means that even when I'm guilty of an offense, I will not receive the punishment I deserve. It is a judicial term in the justice framework of God. The Bible tells us "mercy triumphs over judgment." (James 2:13) Since Jesus has already paid the penalty for my mistakes, I can receive mercy from God and I'm free to be generous with showing mercy to others. Instead of being self-righteous and critical of others, I am free to "consider others better than myself," according to Philippians 2:3. When I extend mercy, I have the other person's best interest in mind. I give up my right to retaliate or seek revenge after someone deliberately offended me or maligned me. To be merciful in a marriage relationship provides a conduit for the flow of positive emotions towards your spouse. In contrast, carrying grudges will harden our hearts over time. That is one reason why the Lord reminds us that mercy goes farther than judgment.

Another strong beam needed for building the marriage house is *compassion*. In Colossians 3:12, we read, 'Therefore, as God's chosen people, holy and dearly loved, clothe yourselves with compassion."

When Jesus saw the crowds that followed him, he had compassion on them and healed their sick. When he saw the leper in his misery, he had compassion on him and healed him. The two blind men shouted, "Jesus, son of David have mercy on us!" and it says that Jesus stretched out his hand and healed them, even though his disciples had ordered them to stop shouting. Compassion says, "I am not only suffering with them, but I'll do something to alleviate their pain." That action distinguishes compassion from sympathy or pity. By understanding the pain, I am not only identifying with them, but am willing to act on it. *Sympathy* and *pity*, on the other hand, merely acknowledge the dilemma of the person without necessarily becoming involved.

The relationships between husband and wife, and parents to their children, are dynamic because we have compassion on each other. We are willing to go out of our way to bring help. A father who leaves work because of a crisis at home, a mother who stays up all night to watch over her troubled child, a young man who aids his brother in a financial loss are all showing family compassion. The pattern is that the qualities practiced at home will soon find application outside the home as well. Children easily learn to care for the homeless, the widows, the orphans, the foreigners, the sick, or the disenfranchised when care has been practiced within the family. James, the brother of Jesus, calls this "true religion." (James 1:27) In our government, it would be under the Department of Social Welfare.

A strategic beam that supports a strong family, is called *peacemaking*. In Matthew 5:9, we read, "Jesus said, 'Blessed are the peacemakers, for they shall be called sons of God.'"

Peacemakers have the enviable ability to understand opposing sides of a conflict. Because of this, peacemakers risk being misunderstood and are often accused of taking sides. Yet one of the names of Jesus is Prince of Peace. (Isaiah 9:6) He paid an enormous price to bring peace to us. Studies about the birth order of children suggest that it is most often the middle child that turns out to be the peacemaker in the family, even though they may have received the least attention. According to psychiatrist Alfred Adler, founder of the *birth-order theory*, our personality is affected by the order of birth within the family. For example, a *first child* often becomes rebellious (strong willed) or sullen (compliant) at his dethroning, when the second sibling enters the scene. The *youngest child* is most likely to be voted as a "class clown." This is quite a contrast to the oldest child who is usually responsible and serious. It could easily be a source of sibling rivalry. Not being the take-charge first born, nor the playful youngest born, the *middle child* learns to adapt to his siblings at both ends. In this way he becomes quite flexible. He or she learns to be creative in bringing opposing siblings together. These family dynamics prepare the middle child for work as a mediator in disputes throughout his or her lifetime.[23]

In marriage relationships, the middle-child spouse tends to show a low level of tolerance for tension. Should this spouse be the husband, he often refuses to take the

---

[23] http://www.ukessays.com/essays/young-people/birth-order-and-effects-on-personality-children-and-young-people-essay.php

leadership role of the family. He/she may struggle with making decisions. Sometimes, to avoid tension, he/she may resort to inadequate compromise solutions, such as letting himself be bribed into doing something against his convictions, in order to preserve the peace. However, since peacemaking is a necessary component in a family, this steel beam needs to be central at the onset of marriage. (*2 Thessalonians 3:16 "Now may the Lord of peace Himself give you peace always in every way. The Lora be with you all.*)

The steel beam that may not be most popular or best known is one that contributes to the financial strength of the family. It is *generosity*. Remember 2 Corinthians 9:7? It says, "God loves a cheerful giver." And again in Proverbs 11:25, it says, "A generous person will prosper."

Living in a materialistic world, one is easily tempted to amass possessions. Often we hoard the blessings of God for our own security. The word *cheerful* in conjunction with giving denotes a person who is neither miserly nor greedy. A father, who is a cheerful giver in every area of life, will not be worried about the future. Hospitality will have become second nature to his family. God, in turn, pours out his blessings on that father and his family members. Children who grow up under the leadership of a stingy father may battle overcoming the fear of insufficiency. They may never come to believe that God is very willing and able to supply. One of the most liberating moments in my life came when my wife and I had sold or given away everything we had owned at that time: house, furniture, car, clothing, appliances, tools, etc. in order to join a mission organization. I remember standing at the airport with my wife and our two little boys just before we boarded the plane thinking, "Now we own nothing. Yet, I feel more peaceful and secure then I have in years!" I knew then, deep down in my heart, that God would provide for us. And in the thirty years of retrospect, we can confidently proclaim. "Never has God NOT provided for us! He is absolutely true to his name *Jirah*, the Provider."

A beam that holds a great amount of weight is *the fear of God*.

The Bible describes Cornelius, the Roman centurion: 'He and all his family were devout and God-fearing.' (Acts 10:2) What a commendation! Have you ever noticed how often the phrase *fear of God* appears in the Old and New Testaments? Abundant blessings are promised to those who practice the fear of God. The word *fear* in these phrases is the same as in passages where actual danger was lurking, like when the ship carrying Paul to Rome was sinking. The crew and everybody on board were afraid they might die. (Acts 27:23, 24)

With regard to fearing God, Jesus says in John 16:8 that the Holy Spirit convicts the world of sin, righteousness and judgment. If the conviction of sin does not lead a husband, wife or child to be sorry for it and be afraid of the most important Being in the universe, how could the second part – righteousness – be restored to that person? However, without righteousness, judgment will surely follow. Is that not what the fear of God means? Does fear not make us want to live in a righteous way? It should!

SUMMARY

Mercy, compassion, peacemaking, generosity, and the fear of God are blocks that don't build fortresses behind which a family can hide and live in isolation. Rather, they are the beams that support an appealing home, open to needy people and strangers. It offers love, warmth and understanding.

Chapter Sixteen | Dealing with Adversity

"Consider it pure joy, my brothers and sisters, whenever you face trials of many kinds, because you know that the testing of your faith produces perseverance. Let perseverance finish its work so that you may be mature and complete, not lacking anything." James 1:2-4

Try as we might, we cannot always control our family circumstances. There are many things God has entrusted to parents for which we are responsible. We are accountable for choices regarding lifestyle, character building, and the practice of our Christian principles. Nevertheless, a vast array of circumstances we face are too complex and mysterious to comprehend. In my lectures, I often say that God is always bigger than we think He is. When adversities come, when sickness overwhelms us, when accidents strike, and calamities happen, a very natural human response is to cry out to our God. He is always bigger than the circumstance.

When I wrote this chapter, my wife and I were living in South Korea. News had just broken that 23 young South Korean Christians, on a humanitarian medical trip to Afghanistan, had been kidnapped by a terrorist organization that consequently killed two young people and shamefully mistreated others. The outcry, not only by parents, relatives and friends of those young people, but by many nations around the world against such heinous crimes was understandable! Many Koreans were asking, "Where was God, when these young people stepped out to serve Him? Why did He not protect them?" Will the *why* questions ever find an answer here on earth? Maybe not. We can only be sure of this: God is always greater than you or I think He is. God is God and we are not. His ways are perfect. His love has no limits. His power and authority are without end. Isaiah wrote, "For My thoughts are not your thoughts, neither are your ways my ways," declares the Lord. "As the heavens are higher than the earth, so are my ways higher than your ways and my thoughts than your thoughts." (Isaiah 55:8, 9)

What is of supreme importance is the response of our hearts to God in a tragedy. We can react to tragedies by avoiding our next responsibility and distributing blame. Let's call these the *Reactors*. Or we have the choice to respond by reaching out to others who are also directly involved. We can ask God for insight through the crisis. After the shock and grief, we can make plans to move forward. We need to understand that what happened was totally outside our control. The only appropriate move is to bring closure before God, and move on. We call these people the *Responders*.

Those of us making the first choice, the *Reactors* often slide into helplessness, bitterness and anger. Sometimes we will get the attention of the media by stirring up blame and controversy.

However, those of us who are the *Responders* are quick to recognize that God is sovereign. We become stronger in our faith. The Apostle Peter puts it, "Now for a little while you may suffer grief in all kinds of trials. These have come so that your faith – of greater worth than gold, which perishes even though refined by fire – may be proved genuine and may result in praise, glory and honor when Jesus Christ is revealed." (1 Peter 1:6-7)

Throughout the years, my wife and I have tried to let our responses to crises be ones of praise and trust. In retrospect, times of testing have been times of redirecting our life into God's deeper purposes. We get a fresh knowledge of God's character and love. Later, we find ourselves grateful that the Lord continued to expand our comfort-zone.

****

"Well," some may say, "Suffering through an earthquake, tornado, flood or fire, or being laid off from a job is one thing. You can always rebuild or get another job. But what about being suddenly disabled and unable to ever work again? What about losing a child? What about losing a precious spouse early on? What if you are left with the responsibility of raising your children by yourself?"

Yes, there are circumstances incredibly more devastating and traumatic then what we've discussed so far. However, when the Bible talks about giving thanks in ALL circumstances in 1 Thessalonians 5:16-18, we can assume that God really means ALL. It ultimately depends on our gaining an understanding of God's overall plan in history. Do we realize that we are living in a world that is still in the hands of Satan until an appointed time? Until that happens, we need to continually put our trust in Christ. Even if the enemy should win a battle here or there, we must nevertheless continue to stand on Christ alone and determine to move forward. He will most certainly give us renewed strength and purpose.

Why does God not prevent bad things from happening? When we get to heaven and have access to the records of history, we will be able to check out the short chapter of our lives here on earth, and be amazed to see how many times God really did block bad things from happening to *the innocent*. Those tragedies which God did allow may become the very tools He uses to redirect us, purify us and keep us on God's track. We can trust God's goodness when things have gone bad, even very bad. Much, much later, we'll be able to say, "God, I thank you for having turned the train of my life southward, when I was determined to go north."[24]

****

Vincent and Patty had been married for ten years and were blessed with two beautiful children, Gordon, eight, and Carrie, six. Vincent was a computer programmer and had worked for several different companies. One day he again informed his wife that he had just quit the firm he had started working for two months earlier. The reason? He had had irreconcilable differences with the boss. Patty was becoming increasingly more frustrated with her husband's inability to hold down a job. She had particularly observed his abrupt mood-swings. He would fly off the handle over the smallest incident. She had tried to tip-toe around his moods, never sure what would trigger another explosion.

His constant picking on the children, particularly Gordon, had bothered her a lot. "If this continues, our son is going to have as many hang ups as his father," Patty had

---

[24] What we can say however, is that all tragedies in this world are a direct or indirect result of sin and human fallenness, as it says in Romans 8:20,22 "For the creation was subjected to frustration, not by its own choice, but by the will of the one who subjected it, ... the whole creation has been groaning as in the pains of childbirth right up to the present time.

thought to herself. "I wish I could put my finger on the root of this behavior." Often she had concluded, "We so desperately need help!" Whenever she had brought up the subject of counseling in the past, her husband had accused her of making him out to be a monster. According to Vincent, what she needed was to put more effort into understanding him, if their relationship was to improve. This time she began to wonder whether all that he had been telling her about his work and his reasons for quitting jobs was really true. Patty finally decided to take action.

When the couple had first met, Patty had been attracted to Vincent by his sense of purpose, his grand ideas about their future and the adventurous trips he had taken. He seemed to lift her out of the small world she had grown up in. She was willing to overlook the occasional put-down, or the fact that sometimes on a trip, he wouldn't contact her for a couple of weeks. This had happened three times during the year they dated before their wedding. Her mother and her friends started to caution her about her boyfriend. But she pushed those warnings aside, finding plausible explanations for Vincent. The memories of those early days of dating seemed to come back in regular frequency.

As Patty was deciding to give Vincent an ultimatum - go for counseling or she and the children would leave - she got a phone call from a trusted friend who wanted to meet about a private matter. What this friend revealed to Patty was so shocking she nearly fainted. Patty's friend told her that her own husband's brother was gay. He happened to mention that Vincent was also hanging out with several guys of the gay community on a regular basis. He assumed Vincent was also in a gay relationship. Patty's friends were so shocked they decided to let Patty know immediately.

A nightmare followed. The families arranged to have dinner together the next evening. Vincent was happy to see them and felt comfortable with them. They had been friends for years: the men had golfed together; their children were of similar age; they had barbecued off and on. In fact, they were almost the only friends Patty and Vincent still had, since Vincent had left the church over the pastor's narrow-minded sermons.

During the small talk following the dinner, Brian asked Vincent whether he remembered his brother.

After some silence, Vincent replied, "Of course, he's joined us for golf a couple of times."

"Right," Brian said. "I'm sure you know that he's gotten hooked into a homosexual life style. My brother was at our house the other day and he told us that you, too, were hanging out in the gay community and probably into homosexual affairs. Instead of taking his word for it, we thought we would rather talk to you directly."

Vincent just stared in front of him, his facial muscles twitching, trying to get his emotions under control. "I have no comments," he finally managed. "It's been a hell of a life for years now. I guess I'm finished. To tell you the truth, I'm glad it's in the open. I'm sick and tired of my life. I don't care about marriage anymore. That's just the way it is. Don't look at me as if I were a piece of dirt. My life's been a mess from the start. Anyway, who knows what's behind your own shiny faces? I'm out of here." Vincent grabbed a jacket, slamming the door behind him.

Patty was sobbing uncontrollably. Her whole life was shattered. What would she do? How could she tell the children? Her friends prayed loudly for her and after some time, they asked the Lord together for help.

Three days went by and Patty did not hear one word from Vincent. One morning, when she had just put her children on the school bus, the phone rang. It was Vincent. "Can we talk?" was all he said.

"Vincent, where have you been?? I've been so worried. Yes, let's talk." Patty was amazed at her response. As she hung up the phone, she realized that she still had some hope left in her. Something deep inside Patty connecting her to her husband had not been severed. Suddenly, she had a flashback of her wedding ceremony. She could hear herself say, "In sickness and in health, 'till death do us part…"

Anger flashed through Patty as she sat across from Vincent in the café they had often gone to. She felt like screaming at him!

"I'm a mess, Patty," was the first thing Vincent said. He had barely sat down. "I've lied to you, to myself, to God, to the church. I was living a rotten life, constantly hiding. People at work would find out what I was up to, so I would drop that job and move on to another one. I'm just so sick of it all. I want to make it as easy as possible for you and the children by finally getting out of your lives. I'm so ashamed for lying to you from the beginning! I don't even know what to tell the children. Yesterday, I met with our lawyer and initiated the divorce proceedings. There will be no dispute. You can have full custody of the kids. But please, find it in your heart to give me some visiting rights once in a while. You can have the title to our house and car. I promise to keep supporting you and the kids as much as I can, but I cannot lead a double life any longer."

"Now just wait a minute!" Patty burst out, tears streaming down her face. "Who's talking about divorce? I'm not throwing in the towel that fast. This is our marriage we're talking about. When we stood at the altar, we stood before God. Both of us made a vow, remember? How many times did I beg you to go for counseling?!"

"I didn't keep track," Vincent mumbled, "but a lot. Guess I wasn't ready for it. I would've put on a big act, probably put the blame squarely on you without admitting anything. But it's too late now."

"Not as far as I'm concerned," Patty argued. "With God it's never too late. If you're willing to begin to change your lifestyle, so am I! Let's at least try."

"Ah...one more thing, Patty," Vincent said after a long pause. Patty was aware that he was struggling, but she managed not to push him. She had learned the hard way. She used to say, "I know there is something bothering you, come on now, get it out, I want to hear it." She had had that sixth sense, that intuitive knowledge. It used to infuriate Vincent. It would make him so mad, he would leave the room, and watch TV in the den.

"Patty, I went for a medical and yesterday afternoon the doctor called me back, to see him."

Patty froze. 'No,' she thought, 'Lord, please don't let it be.'

"Patty, I tested HIV positive. The doctor said that you need to come in and the children as well. He wasn't quite sure, when I had contracted the virus, it could have been before we got married. Yes, I had had several affairs before our marriage. You have no idea how terribly sorry I am. I really never wanted to go into a homosexual lifestyle. I'm so ashamed. Patty, I can't even ask you to forgive me. I can't ever expect it. I know, God will never forgive me. He just couldn't. I know I will never forgive myself. I really did love you. I'll find a room somewhere. I was thinking of moving away from here. Maybe I could just come visit the kids once a month or so."

Patty sat in shock. How much more could she take? Within a few days, her whole life in a nice, quiet American suburb was turned completely up-side down. "Is this really me?" she was wondering. "Is this my husband sitting across from me? Yes, it's the man that I'm still married to. Does he really have HIV? I might even have it, too. My God! All of this is real!"

"Vincent," she finally said. "I don't want to hear of you moving anywhere. You're still my husband. I'm still your wife and we have two beautiful children. If you're willing, we can walk through all this together. Remember our marriage vows? 'In sickness and in health' is what we committed to, at least what I did, when I married you. Will you think about it?"

Patty waited while they sat in a long silence as Vincent struggled to stop his tears. She finally said, "Come on, let's go home. The children will be happy to see you when they come home from school." Reluctantly, Vincent agreed to go back with her.

The following week Patty and the children went for medical check-ups. She anxiously awaited the phone call, preparing for the worst. In her mind she had rehearsed how she might present the story to her children, her parents, and others. Then the call came. A cloud lifted when the voice at the other end assured her that the three of them had a clean bill of health. Patty carefully chose a Christian counselor, in another city, upon Vincent's request. Vincent learned to trust him about the life he had kept a dark secret for so many years.

At first Patty was appalled, when she heard some of the details. But, she thanked God for forcing it all into the open. She realized that for any healing to begin, all the hidden areas needed to be looked at in detail. Bit by bit, Vincent told them of the time, at age six, when his cousin, Shawn, had moved in with them. Shawn was fourteen and had lost his father in an accident. The mother couldn't cope with the consequences, and had begged her sister for help. While living at Vincent's place, Shawn had drifted into the wrong crowd at school and had become street-wise. It wasn't long before Shawn began to introduce Vincent to the terrible stuff he had become involved in. He taught Vincent where to go for porn and all kinds of sexual perversions. Six years later, by the time Shawn had moved out, Vincent's innocence had been totally corrupted.

The counselor led Vincent in understanding that his homosexual behavior was a choice. At that early time in his life, developmentally he had not been mature enough to resist what was happening to him. The counselor emphasized that homosexuality was like promiscuity or adultery. Therefore, just as he had chosen at one point in his life, even by coercion, to got involved, he could now equally choose the opposite. He cautioned Vincent that the physical aspect of these habits of sexual perversion was still a very powerful reinforcer. It would be extremely difficult to resist the temptations that pull the addict back into the clutches of addiction. It would take Vincent's total, one hundred percent commitment to leave that life-style. He needed to truthfully acknowledge that by himself he would not succeed. His total surrender to God, first of all, was essential. Plus, he needed to make himself accountable to two or three close Christian friends.

"I completely agree with all you're telling me," Vincent replied. "I can't begin to tell you how many times I've tried to change, but ... well ... you see how far I got."

For several months, as the counselor and Vincent prayed and worked through emotional weekly sessions, he became able to forgive Shawn and the others for seducing him in those childhood years. Vincent also wrestled with forgiving his parents for not having checked up on him or somehow protected him. Had they been totally unaware of what was going on? Had they just closed their eyes? It wasn't clear. Both the counselor and Vincent chose not to pursue the parents' neglect any further. Vincent really wanted to take full responsibility, no longer looking for someone to blame. The toughest part was when it was Vincent's turn to forgive himself. This is that crucial stage when a person realizes that the past cannot be undone. He now had to bring all of the past to the cross, where Christ had poured out his own blood for Vincent's failures. As Vincent came to the cross, he finally saw how his sins were completely covered by Jesus' death on the cross. With that revelation Vincent was finally able to forgive himself. What a gigantic relief! The power of Christ's forgiveness was so awesome!

One of the remarkable changes in Vincent that Patty noticed, as she observed him through the months, was when he was playing with their son in the backyard one day. Gordon had accidentally thrown the softball too far for Vincent to catch and it had hit his new car. Patty held her breath, expecting all hell to break loose. But, she saw Vincent just laughed it off, commenting on his lousy catching skills. She saw the relief wash over their son's face. It was such a rewarding moment for Patty.

The healing years were rough for both of them. Yet, for Patty it was encouraging to see how Vincent's growing faith in God kept sustaining him. He had become a very strong believer, never complaining, seldom angry and daily praying with the children. Time after time, Vincent's changes blessed Patty. For every little thing, he now expressed gratitude. Occasionally, Patty wondered what might have happened had she chosen to let her husband leave. God had definitely prepared her for that moment of decision. Every day Patty thanked God for the lessons they were all learning in readjusting as husband and wife, and for the time they would still have together.

God is such a merciful God! He is eager to respond to repentance. He will heal a family in devastation just as well as a nation in devastation. In 2 Chronicles 7:14, the Lord says, "if my people, who are called by my name, will humble themselves and pray and seek my face and turn from their wicked ways, then I will hear from heaven, and I will forgive their sin and will heal their land."

SUMMARY

When we feel overwhelmed by circumstances beyond our control, we can reach out to our heavenly Father, who is above each adversity. He is as close as the speaking of his name. As life continues to move past those difficult points, we can look back later in amazement, realizing how God had been there all along. The story of Vincent and Patty helps us know that relying on our own solutions will get us into deeper trouble. Only God's intervention and grace can free us.

Chapter Seventeen | Domestic Violence

"If it is possible, as far as it depends on you, live at peace with everyone."
Romans 12:18

My wife and I have had the privilege of working in countries on four different continents. Sometimes we would take student teams along. We were always encouraged to see how effective these young people were. They would help restore families by teaching in seminars, working in family organizations and praying with individuals or groups. And generally they were bringing light and hope to the despondent ones.

On one of these trips, a couple of our students were placed in the Center Against Violence to Women – a shelter to protect women from abusive husbands. Victims would have temporary shelter there until the courts had finished dealing with a particular grievance or until the domestic crisis had been resolved. The students worked alongside the staff. One of the saddest cases of domestic violence I had ever heard of was at that place. A lady had poured gasoline over her drunken husband, setting him and the whole house on fire!

One would ask, "Why on earth would a woman do such a thing?" When the whole story came to light, we were all shocked. During her many years of marriage, the wife had been so severely beaten and so extremely abused, that she had always needed to be hospitalized. She had, in fact, become quite crippled. None of her family, friends, medical personnel, police, or judges had actually bothered to help her. Finally, she took matters into her own hands. At that time, after it had become an international scandal, the courts finally took mercy on her and considered her act to be one of self-defense!

We have not visited any country where domestic violence was NOT a problem. Stories of abuse have bombarded us wherever we've gone. In some Asian nations like Thailand, Cambodia, Vietnam, India or European countries, abuse stories hardly ever reach the news headlines. Domestic violence is a global problem, in every one of our nations.

And despite the efforts of many psychologists, indiscriminate outbursts of unprovoked and unjustified anger by men, against relatively innocent women and children, are an ever growing issue! Although it is not a recent problem, it must be addressed today in order to prevent worse problems. *The church needs to be first to help,* leading the way for governments and NGOs on an international scale. The church ought to lead the way in any social reform. Why? Because only the church, equipped with God's abundant love, is in a position of offering solutions. Wherever *secular* institutions, governments or NGOs lead the way, solutions based on fear and control are put forward.

The uppermost question is this: Why do men do it? What kind of a man enjoys beating his wife? It has been the subject of many studies in every branch of the behavioral sciences. In spite of all our efforts to come up with a common profile that could assist people to early identify such individuals, domestic violence has not been eradicated. Are there any ways of helping young girls before marriage? Here are some features that seem to apply to most abusers[25]:

1. Men abused as children have a greater tendency to become abusers.

2. Men with a history of addictions in their families are more frequently culprits.

3. Men who have experienced important set-backs in their career, displace their frustration by beating those closest to them.

4. Men with a seriously deflated self-image tend to boost their pain by exercising excessive control over those they *own*.

5. Everywhere, men who have never bonded with their mothers or close care-givers have significant difficulty in establishing intimacy in close relationships. People who fall prey to this disposition suffer from a perpetual feeling of rejection. So to prove their unworthiness, they reject those closest to them.

Who are the victims of these beatings? Are there common character traits that could easily identify the women who might subject themselves to domestic violence? In case after case, victims of physical abuse refuse to report the abuse they suffer. In many instances they protect the abuser, even covering up for him. Interviews of victims of physical abuse testify that they were either abused as children by their caregivers, or had an extremely low self-image growing up

---

[25] Statistics and facts like these can be found on the website for the National Council on Child Abuse and Domestic Violence. (http://www.nccafv.org)

because of frequent failures. They tend to blame themselves for not being the kind of wife that would satisfy their husband's needs. Having been called all kinds of derogatory names, having been continually downgraded by their husbands, they begin to believe they deserve his beatings. The negative message these victims have come to believe about themselves is so deeply rooted in their belief-system that neither close friends, nor doctors or counselors can persuade them to think otherwise. This is clearly seen when the victims, after being somewhat healed from the latent physical results of their abuse, and having been counseled to stay separated until the husbands show tangible signs of change, with surprising regularity return to their abusers. Why is this the case? Willingly, the wives believe the husbands' promise, to never do it again, and forgive too quickly. Tragically, however, their husbands' promises mean very little, so that the wives fall prey to the abuse all over again.

The reason most victims refrain from reporting their abuse is fear. Most often the husband's threats of permanent damage, whether explicit or implied is enough. The abused wife trembles at the thought of what the husband would do were he exposed. Therefore, the shelters that house victims of abuse are often heavily secured. Once an abusive husband finds out where his victim is hiding, he attempts to get there, no matter how far, break down the doors and drag her out.

What can be done to prevent such horrible, mindless abuse? How can women be protected from it? On the governmental level, preferably state by state, legislation providing real punishment for domestic abuse would have to be the first step. Abusers generally receive minimal sentences such as probation, community service, mandatory anger-management classes or some small fines. Defense lawyers succeed in discrediting the testimony of the victims on grounds of provocation or complicity. Therefore, on a case by case basis, victims of abuse have to receive proper guidance to fend for themselves with the help of qualified counselors. They must report each incident by getting well-documented medical examinations and filing immediate police reports. The victims need help in understanding that such precautions are not motivated by vengefulness, but are absolutely necessary steps for any meaningful, lasting help for the abuser. Certainly, in the long run, with God's help, drastic improvements in the relationship are possible.

Simply instructing a victim or abuser to change is never enough. How can they change years of patterned thinking and responses in minutes? Their life experiences, from their perspective, have confirmed them as being unlovable failures. Self-worth cannot even be obtained by wealth or status. The only solution that completely satisfies our questions of purpose is to receive a revelation of God. Only in *Coram Deo*, in the presence of God, can both, the abuser and the abused begin to restore their wounded, destroyed self-images.

At this point, I would like to leave you with some immediate steps to take should you know of a victim of domestic violence:

1. Where physical abuse persists, separate the abused from the abuser. Obtain a restraining order by the courts.

2. The abuser must learn to see his behavior realistically. He will need to be guided through a process of repentance and deliverance, with a Biblical counselor's help.

3. Other hurtful behaviors in the daily interactions need to be identified and worked through.

4. Each spouse needs a mature, understanding Christian brother (or sister, if the rare abuser is a woman) for ongoing accountability and prayer support.

5. The victim must enter a long-term counseling program to deal with verbal and physical damage to her identity. She must take on a whole new lifestyle. After the above process has been 'completed', the husband and wife may re-unite. Once re-united, the couple would continue to need a support group of friends in a Bible-believing church.

In cases where the abuser is unwilling to change or unwilling to enter into the process of restoration, a permanent separation of the couple must be considered: either a legal separation with an equal division of property or a divorce[26] needs to be initiated. Legal counsel will be required.

SUMMARY

When the home that God intended to be a place of comfort and safety is turned into a place of terror and abuse, immediate steps have to be taken to protect the abused. Only then can a process for healing and restoration be started. Immediate physical separation is essential. After a reasonable time, if it becomes evident that a re-union is recommended, it

---

[26] In the Bible God clearly states, "I hate divorce." (Malachi 2:16) But in the very same sentence God also says, *"I hate a man's covering himself with violence as well as with his garment."* Divorce should always be the last resort, but where the husband endangers the safety and security of the wife and children through ongoing physical, emotional and/or sexual abuse, a separation from the abuser is biblically justified, and should lead to a divorce if the abuser refuses to repent from his breach of the covenant of marriage. (1 Corinthians 5:11)

should be done only where there is support from a church, as well as the community, for both the victim and the abuser. Legal separation or divorce is advised if the offender shows no sign of change.

Chapter Eighteen | The Family and Work

"Then they asked him, "What must we do to do the works God requires?" John 6:28

In the minds of many people *work* is considered a necessary evil. But does anyone imagine life without work? Many adults look at work as *that which you do to earn a paycheck*. But if you asked a little boy peacefully playing in a sandbox with his trucks, or a little girl baking a cake with mud, they would both answer very seriously that they were working. Are they working? Yes, they are! Parents may tend to look at a child's innocent play-activities as *just playing*. However, I believe that a child's play-activity is one of the purest forms of what we would call *work*. It is an intrinsically motivated activity purely for the enjoyment of doing or creating something. By nature, children are completely absorbed in what they do. On a child's level, play activities are not a means for getting pay. Their only reward is their satisfaction.

In Genesis 2, we have the beautiful picture of God and Adam working together, "Now the Lord God had formed out of the ground all the wild animals and all the birds in the sky. He brought them to the man to see what he would name them; and whatever the man called each living creature, that was its name. So the man gave names to all the livestock, the birds in the sky and all the wild animals." After Eve was created, both were instructed by God. The Lord had said, "Let us make mankind in our image, in our likeness, so that they may rule over the fish in the sea and the birds in the sky, over the livestock and all the earth, and over all the creatures that move along the ground." (Genesis 1:26) Both of them were to rule over creation and subdue it to their benefit. God himself modeled to them that work is simply a part of living. Jesus said to them, "My Father is always at his work to this very day, and I too am working." (John 5:17)

Work for Adam and Eve had a threefold purpose. First, it was an act of obedience to God. Second, it was a means of developing their unique abilities. And third, it was looking after God's creation with the benefit of provision for daily living. Therefore, work became a central part of our human existence.

****

Adam and Eve had no other person telling them what to do except God. Then, Satan snuck into the Garden with another agenda. Eve's response to Satan's offer reveals her inmost desire. Satan's enticing offer was difficult to resist, "For God knows that in the day you eat of it your eyes will be opened, and you will be like God, knowing good and evil." It may have become their motive for doing their work after that.

Mankind has been using work primarily to enhance their social and economic status, or to enrich their personal well-being. From Adam and Eve up to this day, our wants and egos have become limitless. Instead of seeking that which would please God, and thus be the best for the individual, family, community and nation, we have learned to use work to satisfy our greed. However, as Christian parents, our responsibility is to model a life-style of seeking God for the work He would like us to be involved in. Children learn best by following examples. Popular folk-sayings confirm this: "Like father, like son", or "He's a chip off the old block", or "The apple doesn't fall far from the tree."

Work provides a wonderful opportunity to train children to give their all to accomplish good things. In turn, from the profits of our work, we are able to bless others.

****

Romans 11:29 reads, "For God's gifts and his calling are irrevocable." The diversity of abilities is vast indeed. Sometimes these abilities can lie dormant in a person for many years because of lack of opportunity. I remember talking to an elderly lady who was given the opportunity to take a course in painting. This was something she had always wanted to do, but due to circumstances beyond her control, she had not been able to. She quickly learned to produce absolutely beautiful pieces of art. In amazement, she could only say, "I had no idea I would be able to do something like this!" How many people are involved in work they neither enjoy nor have the talent for? What if every person had the opportunity to find and work in an area they were naturally good at? It would be so enhancing for everyone.

A more disturbing situation is when a child has a recognized ability, but refuses to use it. This happens to a child who was discouraged, ridiculed or even punished for enjoying an early talent. Parents, who insist on their own educational strategy for their children, often fail to seek God's plans. They watch their children become frustrated and discouraged. Some young adults may distance themselves from their parents to pursue the unsatisfying job they were saddled with. Others may comply in silence, but feel inadequate and unfulfilled inside. In cases where a child is gifted in several areas, such as mathematics, music, languages and sports, he may excel in all of the areas. Still he may need encouragement to target an area he is most suited for. Both children and parents have the privilege of seeking God about their careers through prayer and patience. God will direct them when they call upon him.

That brings up the question of how to identify a child's talents and strengths. Several stories in the Bible point to the fact that God may choose people, even before they were born, for certain work. This is illustrated in the story of Jeremiah 1:4-5. "The word of the LORD came to me, saying, 'Before I formed you in the womb I knew you, before you were born I set you apart; I appointed you a prophet to the nations."

So, I'll stress the point again. The *first* step for parents in discovering their child's God-given potential is to pray and get directions from the Creator himself. God can speak to parents directly, or through His Word, or via dreams, or through other people who have observed particular abilities in that child. As parents prayerfully observe their child, God gives them insight into his plans.

A frequent problem my wife and I encounter with young adults at the university level is their uncertainty of their calling.

"I'm not good at anything, really."

"I have no clue what to major in."

"My father wants me to become a businessman because his friend is one and he makes a lot of money."

"When I asked my parents what I would be suited for they said, 'Do whatever you want.'"

These expressions give evidence of parents not providing guidance for their children's talents.

They fail to reinforce their children's confidence in certain endeavors because they themselves may not be interested in those areas. They may allow their own experiences and dislikes of that area to become the measure. A parent may say, "I never liked it, so I don't think you will." Then they excuse their child's negative attitudes and lack of discipline. God is very specific. He created us for a purpose with the necessary endowment to succeed. In Ephesians 2:10, the Apostle Paul writes, "For we are God's handiwork, created in Christ Jesus to do good works, which God prepared in advance for us to do."

****

The end result of our work, the *work product*, is generally something that will provide for our needs. Hudson Taylor, the founder of the China Inland Mission, put it this way, "The work done in God's way will not lack God's provision." In his Sermon on the Mount, Jesus addresses our tendency to be worried about material security in Matthew 6: 25, 31-32:

> [25]"Therefore I tell you, do not worry about your life, what you will eat or drink; or about your body, what you will wear. Is not life more than food, and the body more than clothes?...[31]So do not worry, saying, 'What shall we eat?' or 'What shall we drink?' or 'What shall we wear?' [32]For the pagans run after all these things, and your heavenly Father knows that you need them."

According to Jesus, worry is the natural tendency of people who do not know him. He calls them *pagans*. Their focus, naturally, would be on material matters. Jesus says, "Your heavenly Father knows that you need them." If we concern ourselves with God's kingdom and how to live right, then the things we need will be provided for us. So, what is our part? Our biggest job is to have faith in God and trust Him.

> "Look at the birds of the air; they do not sow or reap or store away in barns, and yet your heavenly Father feeds them. Are you not much more valuable than they? Can any one of you by worrying add a single hour to your life? And why do you worry about clothes? See how the flowers of the field grow. They do not labor or spin. Yet I tell you that not even Solomon in all his splendor was dressed like one of these. If that is how God clothes the grass of the field, which is here today and tomorrow is thrown into the fire, will he not much more clothe you - you of little faith?" (Matthew 6:26-30)

SUMMARY
From the beginning, work was intended to be a blessing to the human race. It was a reflection of God in us, who himself is always at work. Work is a part of our being. Through it we learn obedience, develop our God-given talents, and secure provisions for daily living.

Chapter Nineteen | Streets Paved with Gold

"But remember the LORD your God, for it is he who gives you the ability to produce wealth." Deuteronomy 8:18

In this materialistic world, it is easy to be captivated by lust for financial prosperity. We are bombarded daily with schemes that promise riches with minimal effort. Advertising on TV, magazines and the internet shows us the life-style that is available to only a small percentage of a nation's population. However, it is often presented as though it were available to and necessary for everybody. No wonder young couples have a hard time resisting the temptation to live beyond their means. All too often, before they realize it, they are headed into almost irreversible poverty. The sad truth is, it is much easier to slide into poverty, than to climb out of it again. Often a couple only studies good financial management *after* the damage is done.

Practicing sound money management, should begin as soon as rudimentary concepts of *mine, yours, right, wrong, give, take* have developed in a child. These concepts can be easily learned between eighteen months and five years. Parents model life-skills in this area whether they know it or not. The centurion, Cornelius, in Acts 10:2, is a model of generosity to his family, "[Cornelius] and all his family were devout and God-fearing; he gave generously to those in need and prayed to God regularly."

Effective training or coaching requires long-term commitment until that skill has been mastered. The Lord emphasizes the challenge to seize every opportunity, to train in easy progressive steps keeping an easy goal in mind.

As we have seen, from the beginning of creation, marriage involves a husband and wife sharing fully with each other since two people are striving now to become one.[27] Therefore, financial decisions ought to be joint decisions, even if that means agreeing to give each other the freedom to spend a certain amount individually at their own discretion. Financial management, whether one is single or married, always begins with one's attitude toward God. The *default setting* of our hearts should be faith and in God. In verse 24 of Matthew chapter six, Jesus taught his disciples that serving two masters would be impossible. "Either you will hate the one and love the other, or you will be devoted to the one and despise the other. You cannot serve two masters. You cannot serve both, God and mammon (the spirit of materialism)."

Jesus says that mammon could become a master over us, to which we'd be enslaved. By serving mammon, we then submit ourselves to rules and practices that are opposite to God's rules. Self-centeredness, greed, pride, and independence are only a few of the character traits that operate when money is our master. Most problems of

---

[27] Naturally, since procreation and parenthood were to be key facets of married life, God's view of marriage is the natural one, a man and a woman in lifelong committed intimacy. Attempts to define "marriage" as anything else are fundamentally unbiblical.

ruthlessness can be traced back to individuals who have abandoned their devotion to God and turned to serve mammon. The Lord says in Mark 7:20-22, "What comes out of a person is what defiles them. For it is from within, out of a person's heart, that evil thoughts come - sexual immorality, theft, murder, adultery, greed, malice, deceit, lewdness, envy, slander, arrogance and folly."

Therefore, we must be on guard to first give our priority, loyalty and service to the Lord in *all* of our financial planning.

God cares about what we do with what he gives us. In Matthew 25:14-30, the Lord tells the story of the faithful steward. "Well done, good and faithful servant! You have been faithful with a few things; I will put you in charge of many things." It matters not whether we have abundant financial resources or modest ones. If they are used in obedience to God's Word, they have tremendous potential for creating good for ourselves and others. Generosity, good planning, giving, buying, saving, and investing are all part of that stewardship. One aspect that both young and old couples often ignore is the giving of their tithe to God. We suggest that tithing be regular and that it go to the body of Christ in the church to which you belong. Other money gifts can be given to Christian ministries or projects. Tithing means giving one-tenth of one's income to the direct work of the Lord. (Leviticus 27:30; Matthew 23:23) Tithing in the Old Testament was not introduced with the Mosaic Law. It was first mentioned and practiced in Genesis, when Abram gave to Melchizedek, a Christ-like King, a tenth of the spoils of his victory over Kedorlaomer. In the establishment of the tabernacle, during the Exodus time, more opportunities were created to give sacrificially. It became a pattern of life for the Israelites. In the New Testament, the tithe again seems to be the minimum money gift to God. Jesus points out the "widow's mite" as sacrificial giving (Luke 21:1-4). God values a willing heart and a cheerful giver who gives out of an overflow of love for God. Consider some of the key verses that underscore monetary giving in the Bible:

"Remembering the words the Lord Jesus himself said: 'It is more blessed to give than to receive.'" (Acts 20:35)

"Give, and it will be given to you. A good measure, pressed down, shaken together and running over, will be poured into your lap. For with the measure you use, it will be measured to you." (Luke 6:38)

By the way, once the couple is married, it is no longer *his* money or *her* money; it is no longer *his* debt or *her* debt, regardless of who has the higher income or who had accumulated the debt. It becomes *our* money, and *our* debt. During courtship, couples ought to discuss their finances thoroughly. We spend considerable time going over it during our premarital counseling sessions. We recommend that couples continue to keep their own finances during courtship, but practice transparency with each other. A young man may be tempted to impress his future wife with generosity, showering her with gifts and eating at fancy restaurants, but charging it all to his credit cards. After the honeymoon, she may be shocked to find him penniless! An incident like this actually reveals a weakness in the young man's life. He might tend to conceal other matters as well. During premarital counseling, we generally recommend that should the young man, or the young woman, have accumulated a large debt without a workable plan to pay it off, the couple postpone their marriage until they are in a better financial position.

The process of making decisions that deal with money applies to other types of decisions in the family. The principles are the same. Our priorities are centered on God's priorities and God's values. He provides the foundation of our decision making. Larger purchases, bigger projects, that seriously impact the budget, require the consent of both partners. And once the children have reached an age at which they can be included in such matters, their voices should be taken into account as well. Often, money can be saved when the husband and wife are in agreement. Should a decision regarding money provoke conflict in a marriage, it is better to postpone the matter, gain a clearer understanding, and let the emotions cool down. Very few decisions about money are a matter of life and death. However, should a decision be urgent and needing to be made immediately, and an agreement cannot be reached, the biblical recommendation is that the wife trust and submit to the husband's opinion as head of the family. The metaphor of headship can be studied in 1 Corinthians 11:3 and Ephesians 5:22.[28]

Setting up a workable budget for the family can be fun. After all, a budget is simply a plan of choosing and organizing *wants* and *needs* and deciding what is actually available to meet those needs. Included is a plan of how to sometimes raise extra money. Needs can be grouped in order of importance. Monthly requirements will be more or less constant. Putting things down on paper gives a visual reminder of what has to be paid and where the money comes from. Once we have a

---

[28] The Bible's recommendation for wives to submit to husbands is based on Scripture's "gender realism". Implicitly it is the recognition that the genders are not identical (they were not designed to be duplicates).

handle on our regular income and expenses, we can begin to revise our spending plan as a family. Of course we don't have to re-invent the wheel. There is excellent material available on how to budget.[29]

It is our human tendency to organize our *needs* in terms of food, clothing, shelter and pleasure first, and only if anything is left over, do we give anything to God. How opposite is that to the perspective of Solomon? "Honor the LORD with your wealth, with the first fruits of all your crops, then your barns will be filled to overflowing, and your vats will brim over with new wine." (Proverbs 3:9-10)

Husbands also need to remember to save for the future. In Proverbs 22:3 it says, "The prudent see danger and take refuge, but the simple keep going and pay the penalty." Unexpected events can bring tremendous hardships to families, financially as well as physically. A rule of thumb for wise financial planning, is to set aside ten percent of your income into a separate savings and investment account, one which carries very low interest. A Christian couple's expense column would look like this: ten percent for the Lord's work, ten percent into a savings account, eighty percent for taxes, living expenses, insurance and other requirements.

While major money decisions ought to be made jointly, the spouse who looks after the financial matters in the family should keep the other informed of what is happening. It is best if one person, often the husband, is designated to handle the family bookkeeping, writing checks, and paying bills.

---

[29] An example is by Crown Ministries, founded by the late Larry Burkett and his team. Their books *Debt Free Living, The Family Budget Workbook, and The Word on Finance* are excellent. Also, the material produced by Ron Blue or Dave Ramsey in *Financial Peace: Revisited,* is excellent. Any of these books can be purchased through Christian bookstores or Amazon.com.

Throughout the years, my wife and I have made it a principle not to let ourselves be ruled by finances. For example, when we felt that our children should attend private schools rather than public ones, or that our children should take music and theory lessons, play in orchestras, go to sports camps, play on various sports teams, or be involved in the many church sponsored activities and trips, we did not allow the *cost* alone to determine our decisions. It had been our practice to first ask God for his direction in those matters. Then, we would trust the LORD for his provisions on the follow-through. My salary, whether as a psychologist at the clinic, a missionary in the field, or a pastor of a church, was rarely enough to pay for private schools, music training and the sports programs. Looking back, we realize that never did we have to discontinue the private schooling, even through college, nor the other involvements due to lack of funds. Like so many other parents, my wife and I have made many sacrifices. However, we marvel at how God continually provided for our children and for us as a couple, when we made our needs known to God and prayed about our major financial decisions. For over eighteen years, my wife and I worked in an organization that requires its full-time workers to raise their own support. Throughout those years, we never lacked in the basic necessities. Of course, many of our supporters gave sacrificially, not only to us, but to others also. Most times, we could bless others *and* give our regular tithe to the churches we attended. What a rich experience it has been for our whole family! Often we stand back in amazement at God's faithfulness. How could we ever do less than to give him our hearts filled with gratitude and praise?

SUMMARY

The temptations to go beyond our means lurks around every family in this materialistic world. Godly financial planning should begin early in life by teaching children the value of money. This needs to begin with the parents acknowledging God as the owner and provider of all. To seek Him first, trust him, and know his principles of financial management, has to take priority. Fear of insufficiency can be the root of taking matters into our own hands. Whether we lack money or have abundance, the choice is always before us to serve mammon instead of God. To avoid that trap, husbands and wives should deal with finances openly and in agreement.

Chapter Twenty | Sex and Marriage

"Therefore a man shall leave his father and his mother and hold fast to his wife, and they shall become one flesh." Genesis 2:24

Perhaps the single most anticipated experience for a newlywed couple is the sexual relationship that begins their married life. When the Bible says, "and the two shall become one flesh," the word "become" suggests a *growing time*. Mutual satisfaction may not always happen instantaneously, nor continuously. Suffice it to say that this area, like our other areas, requires the same degree of commitment as training our children or working out our financial unity.

It is important to realize that sex is more than a physical act; it is the complete oneness of two different persons. The Bible often describes the marriage act in terms of a man knowing his wife. In Genesis 4:1 we read, "Now Adam knew Eve his wife, and she conceived..."(NKJV) Also in 1 Samuel 1:19 "Elkanah knew Hannah his wife, and the LORD remembered her." (NKJV) These are beautiful illustrations of a means of deep sharing through which a husband and wife come to know each other in very intimate ways. In contrast, when the Bible speaks of a couple who has sex outside of marriage, the Bible says that they "lay" with each other (Genesis 19:34; 34:2; Deuteronomy 22:22, 25, 29). The element of deep loyalty and intimate tenderness is absent.

One of the questions frequently asked is, "If God created sex as a promotion and expression of unity in marriage, why do many couples have problems in that area?" There is not one single answer for this predicament. Much research has been done, from both medical and psychological perspectives, but I will try to give only a few anecdotal observations from years of marriage counseling.

Some couples have sexual problems because of unresolved guilt. The Scripture warns us that sins have a way of finding us out. (Numbers 32:23) Our conscience is activated by the Holy Spirit and it either "accuses or excuses us" according Romans 2:15, where the apostle Paul writes, "They [the Gentiles] show that the requirements of the law are written on their hearts, their consciences also bearing witness, and their thoughts sometimes accusing them and at other times even defending them." We may try to ignore our past sins. We may try to cover them up like Adam and Eve after they had disobeyed God. We may even succeed in forgetting them. But our conscience will not let us rest until we face up to our past life or present disobedience. Until this happens, we are unable to really enjoy our marital sex. An example is King David's description of what suffering he went through because of unresolved sin and guilt in Psalm 32. "When I kept silent, my bones wasted away through my roaring all the day long...my moisture was turned into the drought of summer." (vv. 3,4)

Several years ago, when my wife and I were leading a group of married couples through a session of dealing with unresolved sins from the past, we were practicing what God says in James 5:16, "Therefore, confess your sins to each other and pray for one another so that you may be healed. The prayer of a righteous person is powerful and effective." The couples had been in prayer, reflecting on their married lives, for some days before this final session. Now as husbands (and wives) began confessing areas of sin they had kept hidden from each other, many broke down completely on hearing each other's confessions. Some of them were very aware of their sexual problems, but had no inkling as to their causes. Eventually, with God's help (weeping remorsefully), they were able to forgive each other. It was wonderful to watch the LORD clean up their marriages and restore these couples to the intimacy that had been lost.

One of the first questions we ask a couple who are concerned about their lack of joy in their physical relationship is this: "Were you having sex with one another before marriage?" More and more young couples getting married these days have lost their virginity in pre-marital sexual relationships. God's standard in this matter is made clear in 1 Corinthians 6:9-10 (KJV),

> "Do you not know that the unrighteous will not inherit the kingdom of God? Do not be deceived. Neither fornicators, nor idolaters, nor adulterers, nor homosexuals, nor sodomites, nor thieves, nor covetous, nor drunkards, nor revilers, nor extortionists will inherit the kingdom of God."

Unless these issues are brought out to the light, they will hold the potential of breaking up a marriage. During marriage, the one spouse may become very sensitive when topics about the past are brought up, worried that the other person may have heard something or suspected something. The other may react to that sensitivity with anger and suspicion, thinking that something is happening behind his or her back. So, keep in mind the warning of Numbers 32:23, "Be sure your sin will find you out." That is why God makes every provision for guilt to be eliminated. When we confess our sins, before God and one another, God's promise is to forgive us and cleanse us from all unrighteousness. (1 John 1:9)

Sometimes, poor sexual adjustment may be like a warning light indicating a major problem somewhere else. Conflicts in some other area of marriage, such as a job, money, religion, neglect, extended family, chronic discourtesy, quarrelling or even harsh words will, in time, have adverse effects on a couple's sex life. Anxiety in one area of marital life impacts our total physical and emotional well-being. Generally, the married couple who has learned to resolve problems quickly, and harmoniously, will find a minimum of sexual difficulty. Conflicts in relationships whether at home, at work, or at large not only bring grief to one another, but they also grieve the Holy Spirit. Therefore, the Bible exhorts us to "Be angry, but do not sin; do not let the sun go down on your wrath, nor give place to the devil... And do not grieve the Holy Spirit of God." (Ephesians 4:26-32)

Keeping open communication between spouses about their feelings goes a long way in removing barriers. Casting aside their inhibitions, husband and wife need to talk to each other about their preferences and expectations in sex as in other facets of marriage and child raising. This is often the neglected but simplest way of overcoming obstacles in their sexual relationship. In an attempt to protect their children from engaging in sexual activity before marriage, some Christian parents have had the tendency to over-emphasize the negative aspects of sex, failing to point out to their young adults the many positive aspects God blesses us with in the sexual relationship. Frequently the husband or wife comes into the marriage with a negative attitude toward sex, implying that it is dirty or sinful. This problem can be overcome with prayer, a good Bible study regarding the marriage relationship, or a book with Biblical teaching about sex.

God purposefully gave the human race the pleasure of sex. Because it is God's gift, it also brings glory to him as we follow out his design for procreation, intimacy, comfort, physical pleasure and unity. It is a fulfillment of God's original plan for marriage, and is part of the blessing God spoke to every husband and wife.

SUMMARY

God created us as sexual beings, male and female, to enjoy one another and to procreate. Sex is an important part of the total marriage relationship because it increases the bonding and strength of the marriage. Outside of marriage, it has the power to destroy relationships and individuals.

Chapter Twenty-One | Love Never Fails

"Put on love which binds everything together completely in ideal harmony." Colossians 3:14 (AMP)

Thousands of wedding sermons have been delivered based on I Corinthians 13. It is God's definition of love. How nice of the Lord to give us these guidelines! These few verses express in a profound way, the essence of true love – the love that most couples hope to experience in their life together.

"Love is patient, love is kind." 1 Corinthians 13:4

The husband of a couple I knew well, Mike and Betty, had bought into the lie of the devil that said, "Your wife doesn't love you anymore." As a result, he foolishly allowed his love towards his wife to grow increasingly colder. The way he began to speak to her was full of harsh words and derogatory sentences. His pride and his imagined rejection by his wife fueled his own response of rejection. He told me later, that it had been a time in his life he now wished he could simply undo. Unbeknownst to Mike and Betty, friends and family who had become aware of the struggle in their marriage, rallied much prayer support for them. At the height of their crisis, Mike and Betty dramatically encountered the

Holy Spirit (see Acts 1:8; 2:4) and both told me that everything in their lives had completely changed as a result.

Shortly after this transforming experience, Mike had a sudden insight directly from the Word of God in I Corinthians 13:1 when he read, "Though I speak with the tongues of men and of angels, but have not love, I have become sounding brass or a clanging cymbal." The Lord opened his eyes and he clearly saw what had been missing in his life: he didn't know how to love! It hit him like a hammer and he began to weep and weep. He asked his wife for forgiveness and he pleaded with God, "Lord, teach me how to love my wife!" Slowly, through the months, he began to change from being a *clanging cymbal* to a true lover.

Without love, I am nothing (1 Corinthians 13:2)

Our self-image, for most of us, is rooted in our achievements. We believe that we are significant because of what we've accomplished academically, occupationally or professionally, or even personally (such as losing weight). On the other hand, those of us who have messed up in many areas of our lives, see ourselves as failures. The Bible uses a totally different standard by which to measure our significance. It is not dependent on cultural or personal achievements.

"If I have the gift of prophecy and can fathom all mysteries and all knowledge, and if I have a faith that can move mountains, but do not have love, I am nothing." (1 Corinthians 13:2)

The point is very simple: without love I am nothing, no matter how much I accomplish in my career. Because all of us are created in the image of God, who IS love (1 John 4:8), we, too, need to love and be loved. Love clearly is the most important ingredient of a meaningful, enduring relationship. The question, therefore, must be, "How do I get that love?"

To receive the love the Bible talks about, requires that we sinful persons be saved and restored to God, the Father. How? By accepting what was done for us through Jesus Christ on the cross. After we have asked Jesus Christ to be our own personal Savior, "...the love of God is poured into our hearts by the Holy Spirit." (Romans 5:5) We begin to understand what the Bible means by, "Husbands, love your wives, just as Christ loved the church and gave himself up for her." (Ephesians 5:25)

"Though I bestow all my goods to feed the poor, and though I give my body to be burned, but have not love, it profits me nothing." (1 Corinthians 13:3 NKJV)

A woman, visibly in distress, came to us for help. Her three children caused her daily concerns. They were misbehaving in school and were in danger of being expelled unless they changed. In addition she struggled with making ends meet with the little income she had from cleaning people's homes. A few years before that, her husband had announced that he felt God was wanting him to go to a specific country to do mission work. He believed God told him to go without his family.

The lady said, she was shocked, but didn't want to stand in the way of *God's directive*. Since her husband was on one of his infrequent trips that week, we asked him to come with his wife the following week. It became quite evident, that it was not love for God that had guided him, but selfish ambitions that almost destroyed his family. After deep repentance and asking God and his whole family to forgive him for hurting them by his selfishness, he again took up his responsibilities as a husband and father. Gradually the family began to be restored. If love for God doesn't motivate our service, no matter how great the sacrifice, it profits us nothing.

"Love is patient, love is kind." (1 Corinthians 13: 4)

One couple, who had come for counseling, had been married for two years. Nancy had been 29 years old when they had gotten married, and John had been 36. It was the first marriage for both of them. The reason for coming for counseling was that they had run into *irreconcilable* differences. They had been planning to have children, but they were wondering now, whether it wouldn't be best for them to separate before having children. When asked what some of these differences were that were so impossible to work out, at the top of John's list were: my wife refuses to get ready well-ahead of time when we have to go somewhere; she talks too long on the phone with friends; she continues to wear clothes that I don't approve of; she refuses to change her irritating loud laugh. Several similar complaints followed. Nancy's list was significantly shorter: every opportunity he gets, he tries to change me; he can't get it that I'm not his mother; he still talks about an old girlfriend; he has little room for me in his thinking.

For the next week each of them agreed not to break the three ground rules we had established together. The first ground rule was that each person would carefully examine the complaint. On a scale of one to five – a one being very important, five not important at all – complaints were measured as to their importance. The second ground rule was that each would listen attentively to what the other had to say, and respond honestly and calmly without becoming interruptive or argumentative. The third ground rule was to agree to not try to change the other spouse during this week. In addition, each one would work on changing themselves in the areas that had caused such dissention. After a month, John and Nancy could not believe that they had seriously wanted a divorce only a few weeks ago! Having become more tolerant with each other, they now gave each other the space to either stay the same, or to change voluntarily, without losing their love for each other.

"Love does not boast and is not proud." (1 Corinthians 13:4)

Peter did it again. This time his wife, Jane, had had enough! She refused to cover for him and pretend he was telling the truth. He was right in the middle of telling a story she knew was a big lie. So, she simply got up, gave some quick excuse, left the group and drove home.

Repeatedly, Jane had told her husband to stop lying -- to stop making himself look larger than life. She had told him that she would leave if it continued. She felt now, she had no alternative but to separate from him, and determined to do just that. She decided to phone her mother and unburden her heart to her. The advice the mother gave her may well have saved the marriage from becoming another statistic. "Before you take that drastic step, I'll give you the name of a counselor you'll be able to trust. Go, and see what he would suggest. If he thinks that separation is the best solution, then do it."

Jane followed her mother's advice and contacted me that same day. The story that unfolded at our first meeting was not as unusual as she had come to believe. When she had met Peter five years earlier, she had been impressed by his charm in social situations. His stories about his adventurous trips had impressed and intrigued her. Only six months after they had first met, they had gotten married. It hadn't taken long when Jane realized that Peter had a tendency to exaggerate. He would try to impress others by making himself look heroic and important. She became shocked to discover, over time, that most of Peter's details were outright lies and the rest were vastly exaggerated. When she confronted him with this, he laughed and said that people just enjoyed hearing his many stories.

As the counseling progressed, with Jane's permission, we invited Peter to join us. Both were surprised to find that his disturbing behavior had had its roots in early childhood. Gifted with a vivid imagination, he had obtained rewards from making up stories. At school, his teacher praised him for his creative writing; he scored many points with his peers when he bragged about imaginary pranks. When the couple realized that there would be no liars in heaven (Revelation 28:8) Peter genuinely desired to change. He gave me the permission to hold him accountable, with Jane's help. In turn, Jane made a commitment never to threaten divorce again. They continued the counseling sessions until they were secure in their new lifestyle together. Peter had finally walked away from his addiction and Jane's trust had returned.

"Love is not self-seeking." (1 Corinthians 13:5)
A familiar saying goes something like this: Love isn't love until it's given away. In other words, by its very nature love is always other-oriented. In loving, I don't seek something for myself, but am intent on doing something positive for the other, as the Bible says, "Husbands … be considerate as you live with your wives, and treat them with respect as the weaker partner and as heirs with you of the gracious gift of life, so that nothing will hinder your prayers." (1 Peter 3:7)

"Love is not easily angered." (1 Corinthians 13:5)

The Bible is very practical when it comes to human frailty and sinfulness. It clearly points out our weaknesses and our susceptibility to sin. It also gives practical ways to escape temptation and get victory over areas of destructive behavior. A good example is *anger.* There are times when we are angered and are tempted to lash out. However, the Bible describes where to draw the line: don't be impulsive, and learn to delay reactions. "But you, Lord, are a compassionate and gracious God, slow to anger, abounding in love and faithfulness." (Psalm 86:15) In other words, disengage, look at the issues that brought on these strong emotions, and ask yourself, "Is it really worth fighting about?" The answer is always "No". Then, ask for forgiveness for any unloving behavior that disrupted the relationship. First ask God, then your spouse, for forgiveness for having been unloving. It is unwise to let anger fester, only to cause more misery the next day.

"Love keeps no record of wrongs." (1 Corinthians 13:5)

Have you heard this question before? "This is the hundredth time you did this to me! Are you ever going to stop?"

Repeated offenses in a marriage are particularly destructive. Unfortunately, these are quite common. People forget or are slow to change their ways. However, keeping records of wrongs is a sure way for those offenses to have very negative impacts. It is always good to remind ourselves of the number of times we have had to ask God for forgiveness for the same sins - often for years. How does God respond to our pleadings? In Psalm 103:12 it says, "As far as the east is from the west, so far has he removed our transgressions from us." Look at Jesus' answer to Peter, when he asked the Lord how often he needed to forgive his brother. Jesus answered, "I tell you, not seven times, but seventy times seven times." (Matthew 18:22) A friend of ours had a gold pin which said *70x7*. He wore it constantly on his clothes as a reminder to others as well as to himself to practice forgiveness daily. This includes offenses committed over and over again. The key is having a repentant heart. We do not want to destroy the relationships that are so wonderfully given to us.

"Love does not delight in evil, but rejoices with the truth."
(1 Corinthians 13:6)

It is a parent's joy to know that they can trust their children. A mother would bring her child to the Child and Family Clinic, because the school principal, or the judge of the Juvenile and Family Courts had ordered the child to get counseling for lying, stealing or destructive behavior. Many times, these habits had come as a shock to the parents.

Since behaviors are motive driven, the question was this: What does the delinquent child seek to accomplish? What is the child trying to communicate to the people in his or her world? In some mysterious way the negative attention the child gets from his or her behavior meets a need for attention he or she apparently does not receive from the parents. This neglect may set a child on a life-long search for love. The behavior, through which the child first gains the most attention can later turn into destructive, addictive behavior.

As we translate childhood delinquency into adulthood, we find adultery, domestic violence, alcohol, sex and drug addictions, depression, rebellion and suicide. Does that sound hopeless? Yes, from a human perspective it certainly does.

But remember the Lord our God, who is awesome, can redeem us. With God's help, no longer do we need to dwell, or even delight in, evil lies about ourselves, but instead we dwell on the truth of who we are in God. We no longer find satisfaction in verbally or physically hurting others or ourselves. Reminding ourselves of the true love, in which most marriages start, and leaning on God for help, will melt away vindictive emotions through the process of becoming *one flesh*. How rewarding! Gradually, we learn not to be afraid of being known for who we really are, and increasingly, we become transparent without being ashamed. (Genesis 2:24)

"Love always protects." (1 Corinthians 13:7)

Husbands ought to provide physical care and protection for their wives and children. God, the Father, does this with us. He protects us, not occasionally, but daily. (Psalm 41:2) As mentioned in Chapter Eleven when Israel was rebuilding the wall around Jerusalem, although the enemy tried to stop them, Nehemiah handled the situation like this:

> "After I looked things over, I stood up and said to the nobles, the officials and the rest of the people, "Don't be afraid of them. Remember the Lord, who is great and awesome, and fight for your families, your sons and your daughters, your wives and your homes." (Nehemiah 4:14)

Our *Jerusalem walls* are the safe boundaries we create for our homes and families. Every husband is called upon to fight for his family. "Remember the Lord, who is great and awesome, and fight for your families." This battle is both a physical and a spiritual one as we fight to keep worldliness

MARRIAGE CLASS

out of our homes. The Bible supports fathers in the urgency of this battle:

> "But mark this: There will be terrible times in the last days. People will be lovers of themselves, lovers of money, boastful, proud, abusive, disobedient to their parents, ungrateful, unholy, without love, unforgiving, slanderous, without self-control, brutal, not lovers of the good, treacherous, rash, conceited, lovers of pleasure rather than lovers of God - having a form of godliness but denying its power. Have nothing to do with such people. They are the kind who worm their way into homes and gain control over gullible women, who are loaded down with sins and are swayed by all kinds of evil desires, always learning but never able to come to a knowledge of the truth." (2 Timothy 3:1-7)

Considering this warning, husbands ought to pray daily for God's protection over their homes: for safety from spiritual attacks and for protection from physical harm, such as accidents and sicknesses. Prayer and supplication should be made for spiritual protection from false teachings through ungodly media. Our prayers might include protection from people with whom God does not want us to connect, but for alertness to the people God does bring into our lives. We can petition God for protection of our homes and use important events, like birthdays, anniversaries or other significant mile-markers, as an opportunity for family prayer and consecration.

"Love always trusts." (1 Corinthians 13:7)

God says in this verse that love believes all things. Yes, true love always trusts! Today people ask, "Isn't that dangerous? Couldn't people take advantage of you?" That's right. That's definitely the risk involved. Trust, by definition means you make yourself vulnerable to others, for love, for advice, for help, for health, and more. Trust is a very delicate aspect of any relationship. From a human perspective, it is extended with apprehension. However, when we rely on Jesus Christ – the foundation of our relationships – we can give room for trust to be expressed. Our trust is, first of all, in the Lord. Only God can fully protect us from harm. That's why Proverbs 3:5-6 encourages us to "trust in the Lord with all your heart and do not lean on our own understanding, in all our ways to acknowledge Him and he will direct your path." Ultimately, God is absolutely trustworthy! We, who are marked by sin, are often let down and often let others down, but we are able to trust to the extent that we have surrendered ourselves to God. Therefore, in family decisions, we pray, "Lord, I trust you to guide and protect me as I put my trust in my husband (or wife or child) for these decisions."

"Love always hopes." (1 Corinthians 13:7)

On which basis can I expect something I am hoping for to happen? Is hope not merely another word for wishful thinking? Haven't we all hoped for things that never came about? Yes. It can be very discouraging. Personally, my wife and I have spent many hours trying to build up the confidence of people who have lost hope even to the point of despair.

However, hope is distinctly different from wishful thinking. An example of the kind of hope I am talking about is in God's relationship with Abraham. The hope that sustained Abraham was based on God's covenantal promise. It was a blessing that Abraham was to receive, against all odds. So the Bible tells us in Romans 4:18-25, "Against all hope [wishful thinking], Abraham in hope [hope based on God's promise] believed and so became the father of many nations, just as it had been said to him, 'So shall your offspring be.'"

This kind of hope does not look at the circumstances, but looks to God, who alone is capable of transforming situations and people. Hebrews 6:19 tells us that "we have this hope as an anchor for the soul, firm and secure."

God doesn't always give what we are hoping for. He sifts through the intentions of our hearts and gives according to what is needed. The love between a husband and his wife rests on God's unchangeable nature. During the waiting time, the couple's love becomes stronger and more patient with God and each other. That is why we say, "love always hopes."

"Love always perseveres." (1 Corinthians 13:7)

Anticipating unpredictable times after the honeymoon, the marriage ceremony usually includes vows that safeguard against illusions of perpetual bliss and ease. The frequently used marriage vows go something like this: *"I, take you, as my lawfully wedded wife/husband, to have and to hold from this day forward; for better, for worse; for richer, for poorer, in sickness and in health, until death does us part."*

This kind of vow requires an unshakable commitment to the marriage. It goes beyond our feelings of happiness and requires perseverance. Persevering through *thick and thin* would drop the divorce rate to a single digit percentage. One-parent households would dwindle; teen pregnancy would be reduced, STDs, poverty, juvenile delinquencies, school drop-outs and many other social ills would radically decrease. Women would feel more secure and appreciated. And men would become more mature by assuming their responsibilities at work, at home, and in the community.

The Bible is very practical in outlining the progress to maturity. In 2 Peter 1:5-7 we read, "For this very reason, make every effort to add to your faith goodness; and to goodness, knowledge; and to knowledge, self-control; and to self-control, perseverance; and to perseverance, godliness; and to godliness, [philio] mutual affection; and to mutual affection, [agape] love."

As husbands and wives, fathers and mothers we cannot stay at the same spot we were in when we first got married. After accepting Jesus Christ as our Savior, we need to 'make every effort' to progress in the Lord, until the end of our days. Love is up-building, liberating and always growing. Perseverance says, "I'll never give up loving you!"

SUMMARY

Every relationship thrives on love, simply because love is the essence of God's nature. The only relationship that can completely satisfy our longing for wholeness is the one with our Creator. On a human level, a marriage that is based on God's, unconditional love will unite our spirit, soul and body in a fulfilling intimacy.

Made in the USA
Middletown, DE
14 June 2015